Red Lipstick, Cancer, and Prayers of the Multitude

Pam Villines

TRILOGY CHRISTIAN PUBLISHERS

TUSTIN, CA

Trilogy Christian Publishers

A Wholly Owned Subsidiary of Trinity Broadcasting Network

2442 Michelle Drive

Tustin, CA 92780

For information, address Trilogy Christian Publishing

Rights Department, 2442 Michelle Drive, Tustin, Ca 92780.

Trilogy Christian Publishing/ TBN and colophon are trademarks of Trinity Broadcasting Network.

For information about special discounts for bulk purchases, please contact Trilogy Christian Publishing.

Manufactured in the United States of America

10 9 8 7 6 5 4 3 2 1

Library of Congress Cataloging-in-Publication Data is available.

ISBN 978-1-64088-425-0

ISBN 978-1-64088-426-7 (e-book)

Contents

A Note From the Author...

The title of my book may seem unusual to you, but it doesn't surprise God. He made me the way I am, and I have always loved wearing red lipstick-my signature color! However, I have also been diagnosed with a serious form of cancer. As I talked to God about what He wanted me to do, He was very specific in His reply to me. He told me that I could feel sorry for myself or I could get people to pray—not a few people, but a multitude! I have done what He asked of me.

What He has asked me to do may be different than what He has asked of you. Jesus desires to work in each of our lives personally. He wants to love each of us personally, as if we were the only person created. I pray you will see my relationship with Jesus and what it has meant to me. My battle against cancer has raged, but His love for me has been unfailing. As multiple stories unfold on these pages, I hope you'll see a common thread that runs throughout every story. That thread has been woven together with God, faith, and the prayers of His multitude. I want you to know Jesus more deeply than you ever have. I pray you will long to have Him as Lord and Savior of your life.

My life hasn't been perfect, but my God has been. I admitted to Him that I am a sinner, and I gave my life to Him. I no longer live a life separated from Him, no matter where the twists and turns have led me. All the paths on my journey belong to Him. This God who loves me also wants to love you in the same complete and satisfying way. He has a path for you. He wants to make a way for you! Tell Him of your failures and heartbreaks. Ask Him to forgive you and make you a new creation. Ask Him to be your Lord. He is ready and able, and life with Him is eternally extraordinary!

Chapter One

For many years, I was a mental health therapist. When asked, I gave people advice and thoughtful counsel on how I believed they could make their lives better. The struggles clients shared with me were often heartbreaking and sometimes almost unbelievable. I listened with a loving ear as people told me what they were facing and what they had to overcome. As humans living in a fallen world, it seems there has always been a battle to face. In those years, sometimes divorce won. Sometimes, alcohol won. Sometimes, sin won, but God stepped in to help them become stronger so the struggle would not overtake them. I was blessed He chose to use me as He worked in the lives of His people. I visited many kind souls who were sick, even those on their death beds. My best suggestions were often simple words of encouragement or a prayer.

My uncomplicated words seemed to bring peace and comfort to those with anxiety and strife. Many were lonely, and a friendly hug or someone to talk with fulfilled their most immediate needs. I believe we are all similar in that longing. In my own life, a touch or hug from someone who I knew truly cared for me meant more than anything else when I needed it most.

I had, and always will have, a heart for those who are hurting. The reality of what I learned, what I felt for others, and what I now need have all melded together. This is my story. It's that simple; it's that complicated. Maybe the better verbiage is to say this is actually God's story. He is the author and the finisher of my faith.

I now own and operate the Amish Country Store & Restaurant in Muskogee, Oklahoma. I have no idea how I managed to get into the restaurant business, but because of the ideas and opportunities God gave me, I no longer provide counseling services. Instead, my time is devoted to my Amish restaurant and store.

Recently, I have also been diagnosed with a terminal illness. It's difficult for me to type the word cancer, much less think and dwell on the reality of what that means. It is almost blasé to hear people say, "The battle is real," but my battle is, indeed, real. I am fighting Satan himself, but I do not war alone. I have my Champion by my side. He goes before me each day and every long night. What I want to focus on is that I am already triumphant—one prayer and one hug at a time-thanks to God who is my Healer and all the encouragers He daily sends to me. My ending was written long ago, and I know it is good, for He is good.

> For the Lord is good; his mercy is everlasting; and his truth endureth to all generations. – Psalm 100:5

I was born in Seminole, Oklahoma, in 1954. We were an average family who lived on my granddaddy and grandma's land. There were three girls in my family, but my two sisters were older and basically out of the house while I was growing up. Sometimes, I was able to play with my cousins who lived next door by my grandma's house. For the most part, though, I learned to find ways to entertain myself, often playing in the creek and swimming in the pond.

My mom's nickname was Macky—short for Maxine. She was the piano player at the local Baptist church. People loved her upbeat style, which now I could only describe as Pentecostal. Worship came alive when she played! The passion came from deep in her soul because she loved Jesus. She was a Sunday school teacher who knew the Word because she dwelled in the pages of her Bible. My sweet mom was a prayer warrior, too. She knew how to fight during a spiritual struggle. How can you not have joy in your heart when you know Jesus? How blessed I was to have a mother who lived out her faith!

~

Going to church wasn't optional with my dad and mom. Too tired? Too bad. There was no cutting a deal or plea bargaining my case. It was a fact; we were going to church.

I didn't mind, though. In fact, I liked church. Daddy had a brother named Cagle Graves who was a fired-up Assembly of God preacher in a nearby small church, called Old Glory, that we attended when I was young. We would arrive every Sunday, and I could not wait until the point in the service when the pastor would call all the children up to the platform.

If you went to church, you could write your name on a small cardboard fish. It was then placed in a tiny glass bowl, and the preacher would use his big hands to grab a fish out of the bowl. If he called your name, you won a quarter. I was more than jubilant when my name was called! I always jumped for joy, and it was certainly a special treat. All the other children enjoyed it as much as I did, so it wasn't difficult to get them to come to church, either. It was a great time to be a kid!

I remember my uncle jumping up and shaking and speaking the Word of God as people came to the altar to pray and be healed. I didn't understand everything since I was a child, but I knew it was genuine. This strange feeling made me want to cry inside, as if someone was holding me, making me feel secure and safe.

My uncle had a great sense of humor, too. When I was still a young girl, he called our house and told us to hurry up and come over. He had a marvelous surprise—a color TV! Wow! No one we knew had a color television, and we excitedly loaded up into the car and rushed to see this newfangled addition to their family!

Imagine our surprise when we walked through the door and saw that glorious contraption. It was color all right. The top part of the TV screen had blue Saran Wrap over it, and the bottom had green Saran Wrap over it. Boy! My prankster uncle had a great sense of humor, especially when it came to my dad.

~

Having company over to our home always excited me. One day after church, my parents had invited their best friends to our house. The adults were all sitting outside talking when I decided to ride my old bike to the top of the hill. In my sheer exhilaration at having company at our house, I became a show-off to our visitors by riding as fast as I could down the hill. Now my bike wasn't a fancy bike like some kids had. In fact, it didn't even have grips on the handlebars. While they watched, I started down the hill, going as fast as I could pedal. I was unable to see the sand that had settled at the finish line, which some might have called the bottom of the hill. As soon as I passed in front of my parents and our visitors, my bike slid out of control in that sneaky and treacherous sand, throwing me onto the hard ground. Immediately, an excruciating pain ran down my leg. When I tried to stand, warm blood flowed down into my shoes. *Well, I am going to die.* I looked at my wrecked ride, and I became aware the handlebar of my bike, where the grippers were supposed to be, had stabbed me in my upper thigh. Without the gripper on my handlebar, the metal was sharp and easily sliced through my delicate skin, into my small, young leg, like a warm knife slicing soft butter. My thoughts about dying weren't too far-fetched. I could not stop bleeding.

My grandma and my sister Sharon were leaving to go to the grocery store so Daddy snatched me up quickly, put me in the car, and rushed me to the emergency room, moving as fast as he could. The doctor said that old bike handle had almost hit my main artery. If it had, we never would have made it to the ER in time, and I would have died in the car.

Even though I was alive, it was technically a large stab wound, so it was serious. Infection was a legitimate cause for concern. The doctor kept me an entire week at the hospital, and my scar from twelve big stitches will always be a reminder of my daring stunt.

Staying in the boring hospital was no fun at all, and my leg hurt, but my thoughtful grandma knew just what to do. She came to the hospital with a surprise for me-a crank music box that played "Old McDonald." It was grand! I played with it and played with it and played with it. That little box of delight was just what I needed to lift my spirits, and after fifty-five years, it is still a treasure to me. I will cherish it always.

Childhood experiences have always been easy for me to recall—fun, important lessons learned, and people I loved. The spiritual times and memories, though, have served to strengthened me. I watched as adults prayed and expected healings and miracles. I knew they were coming to God's altar with believing hearts. As children, we learned to respect our elders at church, and if we didn't, we were corrected by those adults around us. It didn't matter if the adult was related to you. You knew you better mind and respect any and every adult, or you would be in double trouble with your parents.

Chapter Two

My mother truly loved the Lord, but it didn't mean my mom had an easy life. My dad, S.J., was diagnosed with colon cancer when he was only thirty-four years old. Shortly afterward, he had a complex surgery. That was many years ago, and the doctors didn't prescribe chemo or radiation for my dad. My mom and I temporarily made our home at a hotel close to the hospital, because that type of surgery was serious and complicated. Loneliness enveloped me when my mother and I stayed in that hotel for five, seemingly unending, months. I missed my dad with every fiber of my being, which may sound strange since we were able to see him. However, he didn't have the ability or time to give me attention. He was extremely ill, and the never-ending days turned into weeks. It took all of his energy to fight for his life.

At age seven, I didn't comprehend what a terrible disease cancer really was, and I certainly didn't understand then what that diagnosis meant to Daddy. If he lived, he would forever have to attend to the bag he carried on his side—the trade he had to make to stay alive. I will always remember the look that flashed across his face when he became completely frustrated dealing with it.

Four years passed, and as Daddy navigated through the tedious and uncomfortable healing process from colon cancer, he then began to get short of breath. With the frequency of his breathing issues, Daddy had cause to believe something else was wrong with his body. Unfortunately, Daddy was right. We soon found out he had a spot on his lung, which turned out to be lung cancer.

I can only imagine what went through his mind. He had come so far, fought like a warrior, and suddenly, Daddy had to face cancer again. I would have expected anyone to become down or cranky or to have a desire to simply give up. Not Daddy. Daddy didn't even seem to worry.

He was admitted to the hospital to have the lung tumor removed. Once the doctors finished his surgery, Daddy was left with one full lung and the lower lobe in his right lung. From that point on, Daddy never was able to breathe the same. He would easily get out of breath, but never once did I see my Daddy get depressed. He always seemed to keep his faith, and when I think of my daddy, I think about what a great faith he had in our big God!

~

Since Daddy had such serious health problems, my mom supported us financially by having a beauty shop in our home. Now it would be called a salon, but we always called it a beauty shop. It was the perfect fit for our lives, even if there were times I had to sweep the shop floor as part of my chores. Mom, being a beautician, not only provided money we definitely needed to make ends meet while Dad recuperated, but my mom made sure we had our hair done and nice clothes to wear to church. She became a breadwinner in a time when that wasn't typical for women. God showed me what a woman could accomplish through my mom. I didn't know then that I would end up being the breadwinner in our family or that I would own various businesses, including my Amish store. I would lean on her strong example and the work ethic that she displayed, especially in the hardest of times.

Mom worked every day except Sunday. She managed to cook lunch for Daddy and supper for me. She never seemed to tire, although she must have been worn out. I watched how she struggled to do all the chores while also working as a beautician. She was on her feet long into the night to get it all done. She loved her family with her life, not just her words, and she gave unselfishly to all of us. Sometimes I hear of people wanting to change the world, and I wonder how many of us would be willing to love our own families if loving them became that physically and emotionally demanding. I felt as though she understood how God loved her, and her life and love mirrored that to us and to everyone with whom she came in contact.

Eventually, Daddy got through his season of illness. I was relieved and hopeful and glad! He began to play golf and enjoy his life again. When he went through those battles, I hadn't fully comprehended how much I missed my dad simply being a father to me in those earlier years.

By the time my dad turned 42, my dad had lived through two battles with cancer. Anyone would hope and believe that was enough for any family to survive. It seemed that season wasn't over for us just yet. My mom was then diagnosed with colon cancer. This time the doctors did use chemo and radiation, and it was horrible.

My mom's mouth was full of blisters. She could not eat anything, and she said it was a hard battle. She and my dad drove three hours every, single day for her to get her treatments. I could only imagine riding in the car, utterly sick and uncomfortable, for hours on end. I never heard her complain, but she seemed to pray a lot. They removed the cancer in my mom's colon, and she, too, had a colostomy bag, just like my dad. How was it possible that both of my parents had this particular cancer and both were forced to use colostomy bags?

I will never forget how traumatizing the radiation and chemo was on my mom. However, my mom survived another 20 years cancer-free and seemed to be in good health. The memory of how my momma suffered, how she looked-being weak and sick in her bed—is something I will never forget. I knew then that I would never take the treatments if I got sick.

It seems my parents suffered greatly. Indeed, there were long seasons of suffering. It is important, however, that the darkness does not overshadow the light. There were joy-filled and happy seasons, too, and I have many fond memories of my parents.

My dad was employed at Tinker Field in Oklahoma City, Oklahoma, when I was in the fifth grade. That year, we traveled to Hershey, Pennsylvania, where my dad was stationed for five months. Five months of missing school! I am not sure how that was all worked out, but it was a great time for my dad, my mom, and me.

One of the most exciting things about Hershey, Pennsylvania, was the theme park. It was every kid's dream. As much as I loved rides, my mom hated rides. She hated them with a passion, and Dad knew that—and my dad was a fun guy. He loved to play tricks on us as kids growing up, and playing a trick on my mom... well, let's just say, again, Dad loved fun.

The park had a ride that looked like a small boat floating around on a short track of icy cold water. Since my mom convinced Dad to ride all the other rides with me, he persuaded her to ride at least this one ride with me.

The ride started out blissfully. My mom didn't mind it too much. She even let her guard down a bit, relaxing as we drifted happily along. What my dad neglected to mention to my mom was that when the pleasant boat ride ended abruptly, the track then turned into a huge roller coaster!

My dad reveled in his prank, as he stood at the bottom of the ride. He beamed as he watched us come down, amid a huge splash of cold water! Mom could have killed him, but Daddy and I thought it was hysterical! I love that memory, and I will always hold it dear to my heart.

Chapter Three

As the years passed and I entered adulthood, life settled down to a new normal. I married, and we wanted to build our own home. My childhood had been a good one, despite what my family had endured.

When you are an active kid living in the country, life is exciting and full of amusing adventures. My cousins and I rode horses, motorcycles, and old bicycles. We would be dripping with sweat from the heat and humidity, but our reward for a day well played was wading in the cool creek down the road from our home. We spent the summer collecting "rare" rocks from that winding creek, playing with poky turtles that were too slow for their own good, catching helpless crawdads, and all-in-all, enjoying our lives. The fondness for those days stayed firmly implanted in the back of my mind, surfacing any time I wanted to wander back to that significant and oh-so-full time in my life.

It speaks volumes, that in the midst of my family's heartbreaking struggles, my parents were able to make sure my good memories were as vivid as the other memories my mind held. Love abounded in my cozy childhood home, and I wanted to give my future children what I had been given-a home full of love and fun.

Those memories were part of who I am, and it felt right to build our home on my grandparents' land, not too far from the tiny, cool creek, where my cousins and I played years ago. The land we chose was an alluring spot with a stately oak tree in the center of the acreage, an acreage filled with animals who also called our paradise their home. In a way, it seemed reasonable to think it must of have been their home for all those many, many years before it was ours.

The time arrived to get the logistics together for our home, we had one unified desire-a log home. Our dream came to fruition and was a perfect fit for the land. We lived amongst the deer, wolves, coyotes, snakes, rabbits, bobcats, flying squirrels, opossums, skunks, turkeys, and all kinds of turtles. Our newly birthed dream took root, and the animals made our land teem with life. What a beautiful reminder that God is the Creator of all—and He is amazing!

For the invisible things of him from the creation of the world are clearly seen, being understood by the things that are made, even
his eternal power and Godhead; so that they
are without excuse:-Romans 1:20

~

In 1978, we started our family, and I gave birth to
my first son John Michael Villines. He came after three
heartbreaking miscarriages, and we were delighted to
finally carry a full-term, big baby boy. He weighed 9
pounds and 4.5 ounces. He was a lengthy 21 inches long
and born with a size 2 shoe that fit exactly on the birth
record from top to bottom. The cute newborn shoes
were way too small for him, and in fact, we had to skip
up a size or two. He appeared to be almost three months
old from the beginning, and he didn't stay in three-
month clothes for long at all. The nurse commented,
"My, your son has the biggest feet I have ever seen on
a newborn baby!" As he grew older, his foot grew, too!

Mike had a hard time finding shoes. Kids made fun
of him because of his feet, and even adults could be a
bit too direct at times. When other kids went skating
or bowling, he couldn't participate because of the size
of his feet. There were no shoes! Remember, we didn't
have the option to "Google" or to order from Amazon

back in those days. His diligent coaches had a terrible time trying to find him shoes that were large enough for him to participate in sports, and we had to take whatever color they could find—always black or white.

Even with the Internet, not much has changed in his search for the right shoes. He now wears a size 18 shoe, and he almost never finds that size of shoe on sale. Size 18 shoes are never cheap. He still looks for black shoes to make his foot look smaller, but his shoes are filled with a guy who is big in both spirit and heart.

Then in 1980, my precious daughter was born and named Julie Kay Villines, and she seemed to be the perfect child. She would sing with her grandma at church, much to our delight, and everyone would stop and listen. They loved to hear her sing, and then she turned five. Her voice seemed to change overnight, and she sounded like Minnie Mouse. That was okay, though. She was beautiful and still is.

I think God had special plans for her, plans for her not to be a singer. I say that somewhat jokingly, but now she is a registered nurse, always caring for others. Julie has a heart of gold and loves her momma. She even looks like me! As far as her shoe size? Well, she wears a size 11 shoe, which seems to be a pretty solid size for a lady of the Villines family, but what else would we have expected?

Shelly Leann Villines was the darling third and last baby girl. She is beautiful-and a perfectionist in everything she does. I must mention right up front that she wears a whopping size 12 shoe. She and her brother Mike can always commiserate together about hunting shoes. She has trouble finding shoes, too! In fact, both of my girls often buy men's shoes because they are so much easier to find.

One thing she didn't have trouble finding was her husband, Jacob. He is also a perfectionist, but it seems to work well for them. We were excited about her wedding to Jacob, but trying to find size 12 wedding shoes for a bride wasn't easy!

Chapter Four

I have so many quality memories of my log home. It was a meaningful time because my parents lived right up the road. Even though my grandparents had passed away, life there was rich with God's goodness. Summers on our tiny creek had been an adventure, but I didn't know that same cool creek would threaten my very life come springtime.

That spring, there didn't appear to be an end to all the rain. The rain poured down for days. Then one particular night, the rains were torrential. I put the children to bed, settled in, and listened to the weather warnings. The rain pounded down relentlessly on our log cabin. However, around 11:00 p.m., I heard water running inside my home. What in the world..? How could I have water in the house? I looked throughout the house, and finally, I turned on the porch light. I was horrified to see our home surrounded by water. It was like we were stranded on an island, and panic set in! That tiny creek was out, and it was vicious and no longer tiny. I could not believe all the water. I warned my husband, and we frantically made a plan to get the kids safely out of our home. We were in danger of the worst kind—life-threatening danger.

I awoke the children and got them up and around, trying to move quickly. I called my mother, and I told her the creek was out. I trembled as I told her we were going to evacuate immediately. I could tell she was as terrified as I was.

Once we had the kids gathered, we headed to the Jeep. When we approached the car, we saw the water was already up as high as the door. I thought surely we were going to drown. My husband could not swim, my son Mike was about six years old, Julie was four, and Shelly was two. They were basically helpless. I put Shelly on my hip, and my husband had the other two children. Mike was carried on my husband's hip, and Julie was on his shoulders.

We anxiously tried to walk to my parents' home up on the hill. The night was dark, and all kinds of sharp sticks and logs were floating in the cold water, hitting us as we walked toward higher ground. Mother's back porch light was turned on, and I saw Mom standing there crying. I knew she and my dad felt as though we would all drown. I also knew she was praying fervently.

Each difficult step I took held the possibility of being my last step. My husband was in front of me, and I could see him and the other two kids. I was terrified we would be pulled under the water at any moment. *He is carrying two kids and can't swim! If he drops one or goes under, he won't be able to save them or himself.* My thoughts were racing, my heart was pounding, my body was cold and shaking, and I had to convince myself to trudge on, just one more step and one more and one more...

I never stopped praying for the Lord to rescue us. The water was mean and swift, and I was filled with fear. Suddenly, something caught on my jeans, and I felt as though Shelly and I were going to fall. A sharp pain materialized as something went in my side. *What just happened? What can it be?* The night was cold, the water was cold, and the pain in my side was piercing as we continued to walk. I am not a large person at all, and tension enveloped every muscle in my body. My legs and arms felt weary. I wasn't sure if I could keep carrying my baby. I was fighting to keep from dropping her. *God, please help us!*

I remembered the fence that was at the section line. I decided that was probably what I was feeling, but how were we going to get around it? A little way up, there would be a gap where the gate was open, and I knew if I could get there, I could make it. I could still see Mom. It was such a dim glimpse of her in the dark shadows, but I knew she was still there praying for us. I found comfort in that. The Holy Spirit made sure I knew we were not alone that ominous night.

My husband and I walked, step by step, and we drew closer to the light. I saw Daddy standing on the edge of the bank, not far from us now. He got as close to us as he possibly could. As a dad, I am sure he wished he could sweep down and pluck us out of that cold, wet mess. That night was the first time I felt as if my family was going to die, all of us together. I knew I had to keep my faith, faith in God Who would see us through that watery valley.

As we approached the opposite side, Dad and my uncle Rex, who lived next to Mom and Dad, were there. I felt an overwhelming sense of gratefulness. God had spared my family and my life. We reached the shore and just wanted to collapse down. I was never so glad to get in out of a wet, dark night. My parents' house felt safe and warm.

The next morning, all the water had resided. As quickly as it came, it left. Our home had, indeed, flooded, but it was nothing that could not be repaired or dried out.

I have thought of this story many times as an adult. In an instant, everything had changed. A tiny creek that looked so harmless had turned into an angry and out-of-control beast.

Many battles take on those same appearances. They appear big and scary, huge and unforgiving, appearing out of nowhere. My battle with cancer looks like that, but I have faith God will carry me through. God sent the Comforter to walk with me that night as the rain came down. Satan knew my children's wellbeing would be what scared me the most. God was showing me then that hard walks are not meant to be walked alone. He taught me that even when it seems I may not be able to keep my family safe, He can. He can meet their needs. The Holy Spirit intercedes for us when we are unable to pray for ourselves.

> Likewise the Spirit also helpeth our infirmities: for we know not what we should pray for as we ought: but the Spirit itself maketh intercession for us with groanings which cannot be uttered.—Romans 8: 26

My God is carrying me like I carried my baby all those years ago. I am sure He will not drop me. He will fight the storm to keep me safe and to hold on to me. Although the storm rages, safe with Him is the best spot for me.

～

Time passed in the country for our little log cabin family, and one day my husband came home with a small brown sack. He said, "You'll never believe what is in this sack." I could not begin to imagine what he had in there.

As I slowly opened it to peek inside, the tiniest, curled up deer looked back at me with big black eyes. I looked at my husband, bewildered. "What in the world are we going to do with this baby?" I knew I didn't know how to raise it, and there was a real possibility it could die.

I looked at him, again, and looked back in the sack— met with that same trusting gaze. Then, ever so gently, I lifted the newborn fawn out of her warm and cozy safe space and brought her into our world. The baby deer seemed fragile, and I was afraid to hold her.

How would we feed this tiny creature? What if she wouldn't eat?

Of course, the kids were already madly in love with our little deer baby, but it was a harsh one-way street. She was afraid of them, even though they crowned her with a beautiful and sweet name—Sugar. When night-time fell, we placed her on a soft blanket and made her a bottle of warm milk for her supper. No luck. Sugar refused to eat.

The next morning, I called our local vet to find out what we needed to do to keep our new and delicate charge alive. I knew it was against the law to keep Sugar, but there was no way I could let her starve. The vet kindly indulged me and told me what to concoct for her food. I followed the vet's recipe, but again, nothing happened. Sugar still refused to eat.

Then one night, about two in the morning, I got up and got her bottle out. It was just Sugar and me. The house was quiet, all the kids were asleep, and before I knew it, Sugar began to drink her milk. I wanted to cheer. I wanted to wake everyone up and let them see that it might all be okay, but I didn't dare. I slowly and quietly let her eat, making sure not to startle her. After that middle-of-the-night feeding, our deer baby was ready to eat every two hours.

As a mother, 2 a.m. feedings were something I understood. However, 12:00 a.m., 2:00 a.m. and 4:00 a.m. feedings were every bit as difficult as I remembered from taking care of my real babies. Despite her slow start, Sugar began to grow rapidly, and the children fell more in love with her. They would play with her, almost like a game of tag. Sugar was an official part of our family, and we loved her. We took her on walks to the creek to show her where she could find water. There was a barbed wire fence, but that never seemed to concern her. She went right through the middle section of the fence, just like all the kids did. More experienced deer would have jumped the sharp fence, but Sugar never did.

Since I knew how Sugar navigated the fence, I was alarmed one night when I saw her as I drove home on the old road that led to our log house. There was a pack of wild dogs chasing her. She was running for her life, heart pounding, and if they made it to the fence, they would catch and attack her. She didn't know to jump the fence, and my heart was racing. I was scared for her. As the gap between her and the fence started to close, she faced her inevitable doom. Suddenly, something unexpected happened. In a fleeting moment, a mere twinkling of an eye, she did it! She jumped the fence gracefully, still running for her life. She bolted toward the house and entered the gate. The dogs seemed to understand it was over. Sugar had won. They turned, admitting defeat, and Sugar was safely back home with us.

For three years, Sugar was part of our family. Then we stopped seeing her. Several days passed, and we wondered if we would ever see her again. It seemed possible something had happened to her. There were lots of dangers in the wild, and she had been raised in a home, not outdoors.

Then one morning, right at the break of dawn, I spotted her. She was with a big, healthy buck. I knew then that she had other things on her mind. She remembered the family who had loved her and whom she had loved, and she brought her friend in close to the yard, prancing all around. Suitable introductions had lovingly been made.

The most special treat came when she brought back her own baby fawn. She had made it through her life cycle; she had successfully survived. Her life was full and complete, which was what God had planned in the first place. We didn't see her often after that. I think she wanted us to see her baby. She still had her orange collar on, so she was easy to spot when we caught glimpses of her, or she came for a visit.

Chapter Five

Before my dad passed away, he had one season of suffering left, and it would be the worst he would have to endure.

My sisters, Sharon and Bobbye, were older than I was. Sharon was a tomboy and loved being outdoors. Bobbye, who was eight years older than me, seemed to manage to get me into trouble on more than one occasion. I think in her mind, it was all in good fun, but occasionally, things didn't work out as she hoped.

My sister Sharon was pretty and looked like my momma. She had dark hair, dark eyes, and she was an architect at Tinker Air Force Base. She lettered many of the planes at the base, and she created their graphic work. At that time, the detailed lettering was done by hand. It was something only someone with real talent and skill could do. She had never been married, but she appeared to be happy with her friends and roommate. Sharon and I never lived in close proximity to each other, but we had a mutual love and respect for one another that transcended all geography. We were apart geographically but close in heart. She loved my children and loved buying for them when they were young. She never had her own children, but she loved mine as if they were hers, and she treated them as such when she came around.

One afternoon, I was at my desk working, and I received a call from Sharon. Her words sent chills down my spine. She said, "Sis, I'm in trouble!" I wondered what she meant, as fear gripped my heart and mind. I could tell by her voice that it was serious. She said, "I have a cancerous tumor on my brain, and I'm not sure what they are going to do about it."

Those words haunted me. The word cancer boiled over again and again in my mind. I encouraged her to be strong, and we made a commitment that we would pray. As the call came to an end, all I could think about was my sis and the horrible words she fearfully shared with me. This was another attack from Satan, who placed this condition on her life.

I went to see her as she began radiation treatments. She no longer had hair, and I could visually see the cancer taking her life. Even though she had surgery, the doctors were unsuccessful in removing the tumor.

As Sharon's suffering unfolded, I couldn't stand it. It hurt me to go see her and watch as the cancer entangled her. One day, in the back yard, she was talking to a friend of hers, as I stood there. She turned to face me and said matter-of-factly, "Satan told me he is going to kill me, that there are lesions running my brain. Don't feel sorry for me. Just stand and pray with me against the enemy." I knew what she meant, but I didn't understand at the time how much more I would take those words to heart in my own future.

After two months, Sharon moved in with Mom and Dad. I know it was a change she chose to make, but she had been independent all her life. I guess it may seem like a small thing to some, but it felt like another sadness in the midst of a sea of sadness. It had to happen, though, as we soon fully understood. She started losing her memory, and falls became frequent. I saw how Momma was extraordinarily patient with Sharon, as she tended to her needs. It seems no matter how old we get, we want to feel useful and helpful to others.

Mom and Dad took remarkable care of Sharon, but it was grueling for them to watch their child suffer. Mom had battled her own exhausting fight against cancer, compassionately taken care of my daddy when he was ill, and it seemed unbelievable that her own daughter would be halted by the same unforgiving foe.

My mom was heartbroken. We all were: my dad, me, my children, and my other sister and her family, too. Sharon had never been as sick as this. She had always been strong and healthy. She was an active 50-year-old Christian lady who, as part of a ministry team, prayed for others who were sick. How many times had Sharon prayed and cared for those with cancer? Countless.

Momma was perfect—so kind and so compassionate and so ready to help Sharon with any need she had. You could see true mother-daughter love between them. Time didn't delay, and in what seemed but a moment, Sharon was bedfast. Hospice was called in to help.

I remember a pivotal question she asked our mother, "Momma, am I going to die? " How my mother had both the strength and the words to tell her yes, I will never know. Strength of that caliber can only come from God. Mom had hidden God's Word in her heart, and the Holy Spirit walked her through that difficult conversation and time.

There are countless good things I think of when I think of Sharon, but one thing will forever come to mind when I think of funny stories and my sister. Since Sharon liked to stay outside, she made a pet out of a squawky crow that lived on my grandma's normally quiet front porch. Now my grandma had a habit of sitting and relaxing on the front porch, but she would take out her false teeth and place them in a cup next to her chair so they could soak.

On that particular day, Grandma left her teeth in the cup soaking peacefully and went inside to go about her business. Then it happened; Sharon's pesky pet crow swooped down, grabbed my grandma's soaking teeth out of that cup and flew away with them. Sharon sprinted into the house, all arms and legs, wildly trying to tell my grandma about the fate of her teeth. We laughed and laughed-a hearty, old-fashioned belly laugh. Needless to say, I am not sure my then toothless grandma thought it was funny. All these years later, I still laugh a little when I think about it. Now I know that fun memory of my sister was a gift of God.

~

My sister Bobbye was a stay-at-home person—a homebody. As far back as I can remember, she only had one career in her lifetime, but she was remarkable at the field she chose. Bobbye joyfully worked at a daycare with children, and she loved it. It came as second nature to her because she loved kids, and adults who were fortunate enough to have left their children in her care could tell she genuinely enjoyed caring for their children. I think kids sense when someone likes them, and they knew she was sincere in her love for them.

This was a far cry from how Bobbye had picked on me when we were kids. I felt like she picked on me all the time! Maybe it was her way of showing affection to me, but boy, it got on my last nerve since she was older than me. One night in particular, after we got into the bed that we sometimes grudgingly shared, she wouldn't stop pestering me. I was mad and frustrated. I guess the quarreling reached a low roar, because my dad and his belt showed up at the door. After a few swats with his belt on Bobbye's bottom, my sister left me alone, at least for that night. No doubt one of us wasn't happy, but that someone wasn't me. I thought it was hilarious. She deserved it!

When she retired, Bobbye stayed home most of the time. Then around the time she turned 68, everything changed. She was diagnosed with pancreatic cancer. She had a procedure called a pancreaticoduodenectomy, but we used the slang term and called it Whipple surgery. The doctors believed she had it beat, and we were all hopeful, but she had not beaten it. In three brief months, Bobbye had been diagnosed and then was gone from our lives, but forever she is in our hearts.

After that, as time continued to unfold, my dad became ill again. He developed a heart condition that eventually led to pneumonia. He was admitted to an Oklahoma City hospital, but he never returned home again. His last night will forever be imbedded in my memory. Although I wasn't physically with my dad, I felt him tell me goodbye that night. I was not surprised when I received a call saying he had passed away at exactly the same time I felt him telling me goodbye.

The reality of my life hit. In what felt like the blink of an eye, all my family, except my children, was gone. All those whom I had loved in my childhood had been afflicted at some point with the unspeakable disease-cancer.

Chapter Six

Telling a life story is filled with ups and downs and intermingling details, and my life has been no different. Taking care of my children has always been my priority, and throughout the years, I looked for opportunities to earn additional income. My first idea was making scented candles. There was one other woman in the area who made candles, and she had been successful.

How hard can it be to make candles? I decided I would do the same thing. I bought the ingredients for candles, and the candle making soon commenced. It seemed like an easy task to me!

My truth was the realization that anything involving fire should probably not be figured out by trial and error. On the first eventful night, I caught the wax on fire in my kitchen. *Maybe this isn't as easy as it looks!* My thoughts weren't quite so positive as I sucked in smoke. I was determined, though, and lots of wasted ingredients later, I finally made a quality candle from my own recipe. The scent could permeate an entire home. My candles smelled delicious!

Once I had the perfect candle, I knew the candles needed a name. The candles had tremendous potential, and I wanted a name to reflect what they meant to me and what I hoped they would mean to others. After much reflection, Heaven's Scent Candles was born. In my wildest dreams, I had no idea my candles would bring me such a high level of success—after I finally mastered the art of making candles!

My homespun endeavors kept growing, and I wanted to open a candle shop in town, a place Heaven's Scent Candles could call home. We found a place to rent and opened for business!

Although I lived in Muskogee, Oklahoma, my continuing journey as a professional counselor led me to Tahlequah, Oklahoma, to work. Enroute to my new job, I stumbled across a small house on the well-trodden road that captured my attention. The words "bygone days" accurately reflected what flashed through my mind as I stared at that fatigued fixer-upper, which looked as if it was about to fall down. The faded sign that hung over a neglected porch read "Grandma's Fudge Factory." At one time, this diamond-in-the-rough had held someone's fresh dreams.

Fudge...hmm. Who doesn't love fudge? I guess it never occurred to me that the previous fudge business had failed. God didn't wire me to think like that. I only thought of possibilities—what could and would be!

My girls and I were already running a successful candle business, and delicious fudge would supplement our business further—at least that was my hope. There were a few technicalities to work out, but I knew God could make this expansion happen. If He birthed this idea in me, He would be faithful to carry it through.

My mind was racing with possibilities, but first... *How do I make fudge?* The Internet had lots of detailed suggestions on making homemade fudge, but I didn't want just any fudge. I wanted kettle fudge. Kettle fudge cools in the copper kettle before it is hand-whipped. Delicious stuff!

For two weeks, I sat up long nights scouring the Internet for just the perfect kettle. It was a substantial purchase, and I had to be prudent. This was a sharp fork in the road for my children and me, and I knew they depended on me to lead them wisely. Finally, after an exhaustive search, I found a company that sold the type of specialty kettle I needed. All I needed was $5,000.00.

Since I didn't have $5,000.00, it may sound like the odds were stacked against me, but God gave me confidence, peace, and a dream. I wasn't looking at these things through man's eyes. I had my God goggles on. He would provide, and we would succeed. I borrowed $5,000 and bought that kettle that allowed me to start my fudge business. While that may seem like a significant investment for a kettle to cook candy, it is still going strong at the 15-year mark. It is still the perfect kettle, and it still makes delicious fudge!

We mastered the art of fudge, and every single day we put twenty pans of fudge behind the counter. We sold out every day!

My children and I still worked diligently to create and pour candles every day because we also enlarged our business to include venues such as craft shows. One of our main goals was to brand our product—to become a household name. We wanted consumers to think of Heaven's Scent Candles when they thought about buying candles.

Making candles was not easy, but it was like other endeavors I had experience throughout the years. All my undertakings had the same principle at their foundation. I never gave up and stayed focused on what I was trying to accomplish. That philosophy and work ethic has taken me far in my business ventures and in life.

I hired various employees to help with the new store, but it seemed about three out of four of them would leave me to start their own candle endeavors. Candles started flooding the marketplace. Even the landlord, who worked with me for about three or four months, opened a store close to the same location where I had rented from her. The candle business had started to become saturated.

Our candle making and success entered its eighth year in sales. I had always heard that almost half of all small businesses fail in the first five years. We had crossed that threshold, just as I thought we would. God was with us. It was our time, but in one brief conversation, our time and plan started looking differently, and I was devastated.

My entire operation of fudge and candles was operated out of a shop owned by a woman who had learned candle making from me. She then used those skills to go into competition against me. Therefore, you can imagine my further disappointment when that owner unexpectedly asked me to move out. I was stunned! I had worked hard and put in many late nights getting Heaven's Scent Candles solidly established in our local market, all from that little store. I had thirty days to vacate.

~

I always had dreams of being successful at whatever I attempted. I am grateful God put that drive in me. He wired me to love working hard and to be tenacious in finding ways to care for my children. My visions and ideas of how we would get ahead in life all came from God. Therefore, fear was not a factor to me when it came to trying new adventures.

I was assiduous in looking for a building that week. I thoroughly understood I had to keep my business located on Highway 69, or I would lose my faithful customers, whom I very much loved and appreciated. I eventually found a worn-out garage with no air conditioning. Simply put—it was terrible. I felt as if I would never make it in that building. In my heart, I didn't even want to try making that building work. I had been so careful, and this didn't feel right. In the end, I had no choice. I had to rent that building. It was the only option for staying in business.

What I needed was land on that main highway. If I had land, I could build my very own place. God solidified that dream in my heart, and I wouldn't let go of it. After searching frantically, I found just the right land on the highway.

As the old saying goes, it was easier said than done. I was a single mom, and I worked hard-without ceasing. My education was important, but it wasn't cheap. It left my pocketbook with my daily working capital very lean, and by lean, I mean empty. By the grace of God, though, I was conscientious to manage what money I had put back for emergencies. The total was $40,000.00.

However, it wasn't enough. I visited three different banks in Muskogee, Oklahoma, to acquire the remaining funds I needed. Apparently, in the eyes of the bank, a candle and fudge store didn't seem to fall into the category of a winning investment. Not one bank loaned me the money I desperately needed.

Dear, Lord, what will I do now? I have scraped by and sacrificed to build a self-sustaining business. How can they turn me down for a loan? If I don't stay in the same location, I will lose everything! God, please help me!

I was struggling in many ways, and I had no idea what would happen to me or my store. I started praying, and within moments, Pastor B. walked through the door. I was amazed to see my pastor at just the right time. God sent him my direction before I even started praying. God had anticipated and acted on my needs at just the right time.

My pastor said calmly, "I heard you are going to lose your business."

I sadly replied, "I have been to several banks, and no one will give me a loan. "

He looked at me with his friendly eyes and godly heart and told me to meet him at the First National Bank on the following Monday. He planned on meeting me there, and he promised to try and help me.

I looked at him and thanked him because his thoughts and words were very kind and supportive. In my heart and mind, however, it all seemed pointless. I had tried. What could he possibly do? No one at the bank was going to help me.

It was a long weekend, and Monday finally came, but I didn't feel differently about my dire situation. As promised, my pastor promptly met me at the bank that morning. After we exchanged greetings, he introduced me to the President of First National Bank. I felt my fear and anxiety rising, and I didn't know what to expect. My pastor, though, was very clear and precise when he told the president and vice president that I was the hardest working lady he had ever known. He explained that I needed a loan to build a building for my candle business, and I was good for the money. I was grateful, and I thanked God for sending this wonderful pastor to me.

Within one week I had the loan; I was shocked! The $40,000 I saved was exactly enough money to purchase four acres, where I would build my store. That was the beginning of me starting to understand how God would send helpers and encouragers to me. God sent the right person. The pastor was well respected in our growing community, and he believed in me.

This story is important because I want you to remember that God is always working in the background of our lives, even when we feel He is not there, as promised in Deuteronomy 31:6-8 ...

> Be strong and of a good courage, fear not, nor be afraid of them: for the Lord thy God, he it is that doth go with thee; he will not fail thee, nor forsake thee. And Moses called unto Joshua, and said unto him in the sight of all Israel, Be strong and of a good courage: for thou must go with this people unto the land which the Lord hath sworn unto their fathers to give them; and thou shalt cause them to inherit it. And the Lord, he it is that doth go before thee; he will be with thee, he will not fail thee, neither forsake thee: fear not, neither be dismayed.

In addition, my quality candles emitted a strong scent. The fragrance was lovely if you wanted a candle, but it almost completely drowned the smell of the delicious fudge as it cooked in my well-loved kettle!

Change was fluid and moved into our lives quickly, and our next change was no different.

Chapter Seven

One day as I drove down Highway 69, I noticed a sign that I hadn't seen before. It read "Amish Bakery." *How delightful!* I left the busy highway and drove about a mile before I came to a stop. I saw a modest white home with a horse and buggy out front. The simple sign read "Bakery."

It was inviting, and what a treat when I stepped through the door! In the rather smallish room, the table was overflowing with various cookies, golden and browned breads, and pies as I had never seen. My senses were on overload as I breathed in the smell of fresh bread baking in the oven. I bought a variety of cookies and jellies, took them to my candle and fudge store, and displayed them on an entry table.

Within hours, all the Amish goodies were completely gone. They vanished, not leaving a delicious crumb behind! I knew what I needed to do. I shared what happened with my daughter, and I told her I fully intended to put in an Amish store, right there in Muskogee, Oklahoma.

～

As it turned out, when I built my new building, there wasn't quite enough money to completely finish it out. My plan had been to rent that part of the store out. With my new plan of putting in an Amish store, I needed to get the other side of my building fixed as quickly as possible.

The Lord was at work in my life. He began to give me specific ideas and plans to open the other half of my building. One morning on the news, I saw a segment detailing how the homeless in Tulsa needed work. They commented further, reminding their viewers that if they drove to the shelter in Tulsa, Oklahoma, they would be able to find a homeless person to work. That was it. God had made a way.

I knew I was not a woman who had the needed skills to finish the work on my incomplete building, so I got in my car and drove to Tulsa to the homeless shelter. Some might have disagreed with a woman doing that, but I knew I was supposed to. God made sure I saw that news story for a reason.

When I pulled up to the dingy center, homeless people were everywhere. My years of counseling led me to feel that many who I saw were on drugs, some were prostitutes, and others were simply living in poverty. At that point, fear crept in. The realization, of what was about to happen, hit me. *This person will be riding alone with me in my car. How will I find a person who will work? How will I find someone who won't kill me or hurt me or rob me?*

As I sat there playing out scenarios in my mind, a young man knocked on my car door and asked me if I wanted a massage. *Oh, my gosh! What have I gotten myself into?* I politely told him no thanks, and he left me alone. Next, a young woman asked me If I would give her money to buy medicine. I wasn't sure what medicine she needed, but I doubt it was something that a doctor would have approved. Again, I politely shook my head no.

Finally, a young Hispanic man knocked on my door. I looked at him and said, "You travaho?" Now my Spanish skills consisted of five or six words, and I did not know how to ask if he wanted to work. He politely ignored my lacking Spanish skills, replied yes, and then I motioned and asked him to get into my car. I tried to visit with him, and it appeared he could understand some English. I found out his name was Hondo, and he was from Honduras. Of course, that wasn't his real name, but that is what he wanted me to call him.

We drove straight through to the store in Muskogee. He got out and looked at the unfinished area of my building. Then once he had an idea of what I wanted, we started in to finish off the remainder of my building. Throughout the next days, Hondo put in a ceiling and hung sheetrock. Then he finished the tape and mud and sanded and primed the walls, followed by a crisp, new paint job. When we finished, he even built shelves for the store. I helped as much as I could. We spent long days and evenings working on that part of my store. I knew God had placed a homeless person in my life who could help me, and I could help him, too. God is always busy orchestrating our lives to His glory.

Our labor became a labor of love, and Hondo became like family to my children. As customers saw the quality of work he brought to my store, Hondo was asked to work for more and more people in our area.

Our days were fatiguing and long at the store, and Hondo worked hard. When the day finally ended, he stayed in my home, sleeping on the floor with a blanket and pillow.

I asked him repeatedly, "Don't you want to sleep in my guest bedroom?"

He always answered the same way, "No. Me sleep on the floor."

That is the life he knew. It was familiar to him, and at that time, he preferred it. Hondo loved to eat, though, and he enjoyed television, mostly movies. He laughed aloud frequently, and he appeared to be very happy the times he stayed at my home. Some wondered if I was safe with a homeless man staying with me. Hondo never made me feel afraid, and I knew he would never harm me or my children. He was a kind man, and he was grateful to have work and a "family."

Several weeks passed, and I made many trips to Tulsa, hauling Hondo back and forth. The work on the store was almost completed, and things were about to change again.

~

I returned to the Amish bakery and knocked on the door of the Amish family's home. A kind woman came to the door wearing a bonnet and a dress. I explained to her that I wanted to put in an Amish store in Muskogee.

I asked, "Would you be interested in baking for me?"

A look of relief flooded across her face, as she replied, "Me and my girls were just praying last night someone would ask us to bake for them."

I explained that my store was almost completed, and it wouldn't be long before I contacted her. As I left her precious Amish home, I knew God had opened another door for both of us. I could hardly wait to tell my children. God is so very good!

We doubled down to finish the work on the store, and before long, it was time to open. As He had done with my candle and fudge business, God brought my Amish store wonderful success. In fact, it flourished quickly.

I still faced the situation of a saturated candle market and the issue of the beautiful but strong scent overpowering our tasty fudge. All of this combined with the success of my Amish store, which led to my decision to leave the candle business behind. I stopped producing candles, and the entire store would now be my Amish store.

As He always had done, God met my needs. He found a talented Amish family who needed work and then led me to a skilled homeless man named Hondo who helped me finish my building. None of these plans would have been possible if He hadn't provided a pastor who loved people and who cared to take time to help me. Most of all, He blessed me with children who have worked hard with me to get ahead in life.

After one year in business, Wilma Knapp, who is the cherished Amish woman I met that day at her home bakery, said, "Pam, I have to get my girls to help me bake. I have more than I can handle."

I said, "Wilma, be careful what you pray for. You ask God to send someone whom you could bake for, and He did."

She smiled at me and said, "You are right, Pam. My family is grateful for the business."

We have been involved in that Amish family's life for 15 years now. We love them, and they have become family to us. I know if I ask them, they would be there for me any time I needed them. When I met Wilma, her children were young and still small. Now they have families of their own. Time has passed too quickly.

Wilma's girls bake our scrumptious cookies and rich brownies to help their momma out. Her husband's family cooks our sweet and beautiful candy. We have been a blessing to this Amish family, and they have been a blessing to my family. God never ceases to amaze me.

Chapter Eight

Since both my parents had colon cancer and both had colostomies, I made a solemn vow to get my colon checked every five years. I had an appointment with Dr. Martin to get my planned five-year checkup. I shared with him I had been having acid reflux for about two weeks, and I have never had it before. I thought that I might have an ulcer and wanted him to do a scope when he checked my colon.

I went to my scheduled scope and coloscopy appointment that morning, along with my daughter Julie and my grandbaby Lea. Everything proceeded normally, checking in and then taking me to the back to get my testing completed. However, once the doctor finished with the test, he told me my colon looked fine, but my stomach was red, and I had a small ulcer. He didn't seem concerned, and I wasn't either. After all, that is why I asked him to do the scope, because of the indigestion I had been experiencing. He had just confirmed what I had suspected.

A few more long days went by, and I had to make a trip to Arkansas. I left that day with Roger, who is a dear friend of mine. I felt as though God brought him into my life, and God made sure he was with me on that pivotal day when my cell phone rang. It was Dr. Martin calling me back. He told me he had some bad news for me. With my family's history, my heart felt anxious simply hearing the words "bad news."

He apologetically said, "Pam, I am so sorry. You do have an ulcer, but the tests came back, and there is cancer around it." I could tell he hated to tell me, and he sounded so sad.

I replied, "What can we do about it? "

He grimly answered, "I'm sorry, but it is incurable."

I cannot even express how I felt at that moment. Even in my mind now, I can hardly deal with writing the word "cancer." I was in shock, I could hardly speak, and I felt as though I would pass out. Everything immediately seemed to be closing in on me. All I kept hearing in my mind was that horrible word—cancer. I was scared. I was fearful. I was anxious and worried and sad. My family had all died from this wretched evil, except my dad, and he had to fight it hard-twice. It was a bad, bad word.

Roger asked, "What is wrong with you?" He knew something catastrophic had happened. I couldn't even answer him for a few minutes. Roger sat silently as he tried to control his emotions.

My mind was reeling, and I was still trying to wrap my mind around believing what the doctor had told me. *This can't be true! I'm not even sick. How could this happen?*

I turned the car around and headed back to Oklahoma. Roger and I hardly spoke on the three-hour drive back because we were devastated.

How in the world will I tell the kids? They had witnessed both of my sisters dying from cancer, and overwhelming dread crushed my heart. They would struggle to believe and have faith after watching both of my sisters fight their fights and then pass away. *This can't be happening!*

My son's daughter, Logann, is twenty years old and lives with me while she attends college. Everyone thinks Logann and I look alike, and we do!

Julie's daughter, Lea, was five years old when the doctor gave me the life-changing news. She was named after Lea in the Bible.

As I mentioned, Shelly is married to Jacob, and they live next door to me. Kylee is their daughter.

Since Shelly was next door, I went to see her first and told her what I had found out. She was devastated. I was equally devastated watching her heart break. There was nothing good about this news. We cried and held each other remembering the harrowing road—remembering the outcome and where that road led each time someone we loved started down the path.

Julie, who is a register nurse, knows a great deal about the medical field. She called me, and we talked on the phone. She was torn as she listened to me, and I knew her mind went to her thoughts about the cancer and the outcome. I knew she would have to process things in her own way.

My son Mike works with me at my Amish store in Muskogee, Oklahoma, and we talked the next day. Mike is a large-framed man who is 6 ft. 4, and he doesn't show his emotions easily. He could hardly talk to me about the situation because his eyes were filled with tears. He took the news hard, and I could see the heartbreak on his face. He felt crushed. We all did.

~

Every family has its issues, and our family has not been immune. I don't believe a family exists that hasn't had struggles. Those struggles, however, haven't changed the fact that my children and I have been close, especially since I have been so ill these last six weeks. My children have teamed up to help me because I haven't been able to work at the store, but my children have been covering for me.

A little four-letter word may contain the most difficult concept in the world—love. When my children were small, because of the havoc of divorce, I felt they missed experiencing a true family-type of love. Even though the greatest commandment is to love one another, love is a verb. We may proclaim love for others, and they may speak of their love for us, but without action, love will feel insufficient—as if we are not loved enough.

After years as a counselor, having worked with all kinds of relationships, I know people are starved to death for love. Love should not be taken lightly. People need to both feel and express love.

Some of us have never felt the expression of love in our lives. I know now, that in this process of illness, I have seen divine love from my children. We have bonded even more closely. To love others, though, you must love yourself. That is tough when I was so aware of where I had failed my children and messed up in my life by living outside of the will of God. I didn't love myself. God has forgiven me, and I am grateful my time apart from God's ways was but for a season. It just seems that sometimes we are hurt so badly by others that we retreat and we throw up guards to hide and protect our feelings and emotions. My children can feel my arms wrapped around their very souls, and I am grateful to be able to show them how much I love them.

My grandkids are remarkable. I know we all think that, but guess what? Mine really are.

When Kylee was born, she had the greatest determination in a child that I had ever seen. But then, I had to take a good look at her mother, Shelly, and her daddy, Jacob. They don't understand how she has such great determination, but she is just like them—strong-minded and a perfectionist. That is the Leed family to a tee! Tiger was Shelly's nickname as a child, and now her little Kylee could have that same name! I'm very proud of my daughter Shelly and her husband, Jacob, whom I admire like a son. He has been a perfect son-in-law, and his family has been top-notch. I have never met a nicer bunch of Christian people, especially his mother, Karen Leeds. I have been so blessed!

Then my daughter Julie had Lea. She is the sweet little blonde-headed girl who never misses anything. She is exceptionally smart. Her mother has been that way all her life, and when Julie does something, she does it right the first time. Julie has given of her time to people as a nurse, but more than that, she has gone above and beyond to love people. There is that word—that verb—again.

The emptiness Julie has felt with her own father couldn't keep her from being driven to love others. She has always had a way of making others love her, as she fills them with kindness. Lea's father Wes is one who has taken his life seriously, and he has devoted every spare moment to his daughter, Lea. Wes has been trying to fill Lea's life with love and security, providing the sense that he will always be there for her.

My oldest granddaughter is Logann, but I have missed out on precious years of her life until she came to work for me. Thankfully, she is also living with me as she goes to school. What a beautiful lady! Yet coming from divorced parents, she felt the syndrome of the love bug, too. She wanted to be loved and reached out to receive love from others and has had feelings of wanting a relationship to fill in the voids in her heart and life.

Logann's dad, Mike, has searched for love his entire life. He thought so much of his grandma. I have always thought he has kept looking for that special person who has been molded in a manner similar to her, holding to her values. Our grandparents can set values for us when we are still children.

If everyone could lay down hurts and just give love and hugs, we would be happier. We all seek love and want to give love with just the right person. Logann is smart, and she has had to be strong in her life. She has started seeing that she can control her own destiny!

As we transition into adulthood, we realize there are things we missed out on as kids, so we try to compensate with our children to make up for those deficiencies we had in our childhood years. I think that is a good mindset for parents. After all, none of us had perfect childhoods, but many children were not shown love. Both children and adults may go through life seeking love, making bad choices just to have anyone hold them and tell them they are loved.

I speak divine promises over my children and grandkids. When you pray, pray for angels to protect them all the days of their lives. Pray prosperity and speak happiness and love over each of them.

That day in January of 2018, my path had taken another unexpected turn. This turn had changed our lives forever when I was diagnosed with stomach cancer. I have prayed that I am the lucky one who beats it. It has been a war in my mind each day as Satan has continued to press in to attack me. Sharon's words have become my truth. Satan wants to take me out. Satan has repeatedly reminded me that he spared no one in my family. He has tried to convince me that he won in the end. In my mind, he has played back every negative word spoken to me, like a video stuck on a loop with no way to push stop. There has been an extensive list of kind and encouraging people who have meant well, but they have had no idea how their words have affected my exhausted and anxious mind—both positively and negatively. Maybe that is one more reason God has warned us about our tongues:

> Death and life [are] in the power of the tongue: and they that love it shall eat the fruit thereof.—Proverbs 18:21

However, their negative words are not my truth, and Satan's accusations and threats do not get to win either. God is truth. The members of my family who are no longer here with me are safe and sound, tucked in the arms of Jesus. They are healthy. They are happy. Therefore, I am choosing truth. I am choosing hope. At one full year since my diagnosis, my cancer was miraculously encapsulated. That is the story I want you to remember. I want you to see God in the details. I want you to understand what prayer means to God. I want you to walk this walk with me, but I will need every single prayer you can offer up as I withstand this season, because withstand it I will. God gave me a clear path, and I am on it.

Chapter Nine

As we processed the terrible news I had received, the kids and I talked more about what to do. Knowing we were up against a formidable enemy, we decided to get a second opinion.

Off to Tulsa the girls and I went. We headed to the Cancer Treatment Center in Tulsa, OK. It was close and well respected in the cancer treatment industry.

We were able to get an appointment with the oncologist the next week. As we approached the clinic, my body and mind and heart wanted to recoil. I could hardly stand to even get near the building. I did not want to go inside, and I felt overwhelmed as we approached the entrance. It felt foreboding.

I tried to be strong for my girls, but I hated this place. Not one fiber of my body wanted to be there. I had already lost so much—so many—to cancer. I did not feel anything good was going to happen. I wanted to delay this sickness from capturing one more moment. Once I walked in, there was no turning back, even though I knew I was already on the road marked cancer.

I stepped in and went to the clean and neat counter to check in. A woman efficiently handed me some paperwork, as if this were a regular doctor's visit, and I sat down with that hard brown clipboard and began to fill out the necessary forms.

Then we found the waiting room where we were told to wait-just patiently wait. How out of place and inappropriate it felt, and I felt anything and everything but patient. I looked around at the people who were there. Had they dreaded walking in the door the same as I had dreaded it? Had they filled out their medical forms, filled out their insurance forms, and checked all the appropriate boxes? All my eyes could see was hopelessness, being worn as a uniform that seemed to have been handed out to each and every person who entered the door-people without hope, people with chemo bags hanging from their waists, and people with no hair and ghastly sadness on their faces.

It was more than I could withstand. I wanted to leave. I *really, really* wanted to leave. My daughter Shelly was feeling the same way as we approached the room to see the new doctor. I felt there was a darkness over this facility. That might have been because there was so much sickness there. I went there because I had heard good things about the facility, but I stopped and prayed because I could not shake that ominous feeling.

Lord, if I could just have one gift, it would be to heal people in Your name. My, oh, my! The powerful whisper of Jesus' name could travel throughout the building, through the walls, and through the hearts and bodies of people and make them whole. I just knew it. I believed in Him.

Julie appeared calm and seemed to handle it better than Shelly or me. She was used to the efficient, if not sometimes cold-hearted, medical industry. Meanwhile, Shelly and I were both suffering from anxiety and could not escape the feeling of wanting to flee. In a few moments, the doctor came in and started asking me some pointed questions. He made it quite clear the only plan I had was to have chemo and radiation and to have my cancerous stomach removed. He also made it very clear that if I waited three months and did not follow his plan quickly then there would be no one who could help me.

I prepared for what I would say to him, and I told him I wanted to go to MD Anderson, and he understood. However, he reminded me again how the clock was ticking on the three-month window for treatment. I again acknowledged what he said, and then we left.

We felt lost, and we needed to regroup. We needed to be strategic in our next plan of attack against this foe. The girls were quiet, but I knew their minds were racing as we got in the car. When we sat down in the restaurant to eat, we talked about our options. Devastation seemed to overshadow every thought, every word, and every emotion we had. No scenario we entertained was good at this point.

~

After our long and trying day, I finally returned home for the evening, and I prayed fervently to God. I could not understand why this had happened to me. I know every patient who gets diagnosed with a terminal illness must feel the same way. My family had been through this many times, and still, I never believed I would walk their same road. I believed God would protect me from such an unnecessary and painful event, so I struggled even more when this happened to me. After all the experiences I had been through, after all my children had been through, why? Why was God allowing me to be directed down this path? *God, I'm asking you these questions, and I need answers!*

Then it came to me. God didn't put this on me; Satan did.

The thief cometh not, but for to steal, and
to kill, and to destroy: I am come that they
might have life, and that they might have it
more abundantly.—John 10:10

After all, he is the one who is out to kill, steal, and
destroy. I knew I needed to learn how to fight him.

I shall not die, but live, and declare the works
of the Lord.—Psalm 118:17
Ye are of God, little children, and have overcome them: because greater is he that is in
you, than he that is in the world.—1 John 4:4

I got angry at the enemy, and I asked God to fight
with me. I pressed into God and started praying, as I
had watched my mother do so many times before. After
a week or so, while praying, I sensed God speaking to
me.

He said, "You can sit home and feel sorry for yourself, or you can get people to pray-not a few but a multitude." The word *multitude* stood out in my mind.

God, is that really You? My tired but prayed-up mind
wondered why He used the word "multitude." Later
that evening, I asked God about what He said. *Why the
multitude?*

His reply was clear, maybe so clear because of what His Word says.

> For where two or three are gathered together in my name, there am I in the midst of them.—Matthew 18:20

He said, "People will pray for you for a while, and then they will forget you, just like they do me. It will take a refreshing of people, a continuance of new people, who will have you on their minds. The others will forget quickly. Keep sending out letters and keep your face before people." I knew this was nothing that would ever have crossed my mind, and I was sure it was God speaking to me.

I knew God put me in the hearts of people. I got on Facebook and ask people to pray for me. I told them my diagnoses and what God had said to me. There were many who commented on my Facebook page, and many began sharing my post. I also became a member of the Assembly of God forum on Facebook. They have about 12,000 members, and I asked for prayer and told them God told me to get a "multitude."

Chapter Ten

The events and people who entered my life were an example of God's love and faith. I met so many wonderful people on the AG forum page on Facebook. I knew these people genuinely cared about me. They reached out through Facebook, and some even messaged me to talk and text one-on-one.

Then my road took a detour. It was still on Cancer Street, but it was God's detour. I had a new plan, a new path, and new fire in my spirit! First, I created a flier with my picture and story, and I asked anyone who read it to pray for me. I asked for any who received it or read it to share it with others, and I reminded them to let their friends know I was asking for a multitude to pray, as God had required me to do. I mailed out about 3000 letters that ended up all over the United States.

It is hard work. I know people lovingly want to help me, but it is what God asked me to do. It is my affliction, and I need to keep pursuing what God told me to do.

The first call I got was from an Assembly of God pastor named Don McGraw from around New York City. I couldn't believe it when he called me at 7 a.m. in the morning. It was 6:00 a.m. in New York. He said, "Pam, I got your letter here at my church, and we have a prayer wall. We added your name to it." After chatting, he prayed with me, and we shared and laughed together. He made my day. It was so encouraging to know someone was praying for me.

After his call, other calls started to pour in. There were so many that remembering all the names seems impossible, but one who comes to mind is the Nuggent family from Louisiana. Danny and Linda pastor a church there. Linda and I met on the Assembly of God forum, and then we texted a couple of times. She said they pastored a small church in Louisiana. It wasn't long before she texted me and said, "We are coming to Oklahoma to pray for you."

I said, "Linda, that is a long way for you to drive."

She didn't hesitate. She said, "It's five hours, but we are coming, and we want to pray for you."

My goodness! I had never felt this kind of an out-pouring of love from people. It had to be God placing me on their minds and hearts. The next week they came, and I met them in a motel, close to my store. They prayed for my complete healing, and they met my family. Of course, we all loved our new friends. I think they encouraged my kids as much as they did me. Months have passed since we have spoken, but that is how God works. He keeps sending others to pray, people who call or someone new for me to meet.

~

In the meantime, our appointment at MD Anderson quickly approached. We were ready to get a second opinion, and we headed to Houston. Houston was tough.

Flying was new to me, and I was already stressed and anxious. Other than a short flight my uncle took me on as a small child on his little plane, I had never flown. Even then, my uncle took me up and flew in circles, which scared me to death. He thought it was funny, but for a five-year-old girl, it wasn't. It created a fear of flying that I could not shake. I swore I would never get in a plane again, but here I was-flying. It was another problem cancer created. No cancer meant no flying, but cancer took away that choice.

My daughter Julie made the reservations for me to fly because driving wasn't an option, as it would have taken too long. Shelly, my youngest, diligently made all the medical appointments over the phone and believed if she could get me in, then someone could do a miracle on her momma. She worked frantically every single day, trying to get MD Anderson to get me in quickly. I hated the thought of going, and I did not hold the optimistic viewpoint that my children did. The dismal outcome seemed inevitable to me, but I had to do it. I had to go and see what the new doctor would say. My kids would never be okay if they didn't know I went to have that meeting.

It seems when you go through a trauma, you find a strength, that up until now, has stayed hidden inside of you. Most of that strength is being strong-minded and telling yourself God will help you.

When my daughter Julie made our reservations for MD Anderson, I was grateful, but once again, I was nervous about going. I was afraid of their advice and opinions and what they might say about my illness.

I posted in Facebook on the Assembly of God forum that day. I saw a man on the page named Shawn McMillian. He was an evangelist, and I messaged him through Facebook and asked him to please pray for me.

Shawn immediately replied and mentioned it was odd I had reached out to him like this, at this time.

Never had anyone been so direct with me. He followed his comments almost immediately with a phone call, and he prayed for me. He then asked, "How far are you from Okay, Oklahoma?"

I answered, "About 15 minutes."

He said, "My wife and I will be trying out for the pastor position for a church in Okay next Sunday."

I was thrilled. I said, "Shawn, I will get to meet you and your wife, and you will be staying just five minutes from my restaurant!" I was, indeed, excited and he was, too. We made definite plans to meet that next week.

Then another bittersweet call came few days later. My daughter Julie said, "Mom, I got your appointment at MD Anderson."

"When?"

"It is next week on Friday, Saturday, and Sunday."

I was disappointed. I knew I would miss Shawn and his wife, Amy. I reluctantly called to let Shawn and Amy know that I had to miss our meeting. Of course, we were all let down. I think they were as disappointed as I was. Their promise of a visit was the pick-me-up that I needed so badly. It was a slice of joy and hope in a dark time.

The following week, my daughter Julie called back. She said, "Mom, guess what? Our flight to Houston just got canceled."

"Why?"

"Our flight was the only plane canceled. The airline had to pick some people up who were left stranded, and they are sending our plane to get them."

I immediately called Shawn. "Shawn, God canceled my flight to MD Anderson. I will get to meet you and Amy this week!" We were all so happy.

Before I knew it, Shawn and Amy came to my Amish store. We talked and prayed and laughed and cried, as if we had been family for years. I knew God had provided them for me.

On Sunday at church, Shawn spoke, and he allowed me to testify to the people and ask them to pray for me. Later in the service, a 45-year-old man rededicated his life and said he wanted off drugs. I was filled with joy, even in the midst of my situation. My reality was that God has always been busy with His plans and His desires and His love. We were happy.

My children met Shawn and Amy, and it felt as if our two families melded into one, as if we had known each other forever. I called our meeting a divine appointment. It was divinely ordained that I met Shawn and

Amy. Shawn became a great prayer warrior for me and called me weekly.

~

We finally got our appointment for Houston the next week, and I dreaded the flight and the entire thought of being away from my family. Fortunately, I didn't have to make the trip alone.

When we arrived at the airport, terror gripped me. I wanted to be brave for Julie and my friend and bodyguard, Roger. In a large city where we knew no one and nothing about the area, it seemed like a man could be of help, so I allowed him to go. It was nice to have both Julie and Roger because I didn't want Julie to be by herself while the doctors performed all those tests on me. I knew Shelly wanted to come with us, but she had baby Kylee, and it was too hard on her.

I didn't know what I faced on this trip or what unsavory choices I would have to make. Even though I was scared when we got on the plane, but it wasn't bad at all. The fear of flying had built up in my mind all these years. Fear held me as a prisoner, and it kept me from traveling. I found out that I love flying! I felt peace washing over me. I think God helped me to run to the roar. That simply means when you are afraid, run into what you are afraid of, and you will conquer it.

I believe I conquered the fear of flying. One anxiety down. What about the other anxiety? Anyone who is diagnosed with a terminal disease will have anxiety—maybe even crippling anxiety. None of us want to die. We all want to live and be healthy and work and be with our families. I was in that group. I still am. I want to live.

Lord, I will live and not die! Do you hear me, Lord? YOU promised Hezekiah fifteen extra years when you told him he would die. You gave him fifteen more years, Lord. I want fifteen more years to be with my family. I want to see my grandkids grow up, and my children need me. I am their stronghold. Their father is not in the picture, and our family is deceased. What will my children do, Lord? You can't leave them alone with no one to pray for them or to watch over them!

When we arrived at MD Anderson, it was an overwhelming hospital. It was huge, and the entrance looked like we were pulling up at a major airport. The hustle and bustle and activity never stopped. All four traffic lanes were filled with all kinds of people, all denominations, and all ages—a diverse crowd, reminding us that cancer is no respecter of any person.

Even though I didn't want to be there, I always tried to be nice to people, and I tried to see why they were there.

We stayed at an older hotel, and there was an elderly man who shuttled us on the hotel van from the hospital and back many times a day. He had a kind face, and he was full of the Lord. He would sing and praise God most of the time. He made my stay more comfortable, and I felt peace on my drive. Again, God provided for me. He would always tell me, "Sis, you're going to make it." Somehow, I believed him.

I also met a lady on Facebook named Connie Driver, who was from Texas, and we texted back and forth a few times. She asked me when I was going to be in Houston, and I gave her the dates. She let me know she was going to come in person to meet me and pray for me. Connie said God told her to come to me, and she would be there that afternoon when I finished my test.

I could not believe it! God sent me another encourager. Connie lived two hours away, and true to her word, when my test ended, she was there. We instantly loved each other. Connie continued to pray for me, and she kept telling me how to survive all the negativity I had been involved in, negativity that seemed to be unending. I loved her. She had her doctorate degree, and she was married to a successful dentist. I knew Connie had a busy life, but she made time to come and meet me in Houston. I will always be grateful.

One evening, I met another interesting man while riding the shuttle van. My daughter Julie and I went to the local taco place to eat. We noticed there was a decent-looking older man sitting at the front of the van, talking to a younger man who seemed more of an annoyance than anything else. It appeared as if the younger passenger was getting on the older gentleman's nerves. We listened, and the conversation sounded a little distraught from the older passenger's voice, who appeared agitated. As the driver let us off, we all scattered and went our own way, and we returned to catch the bus in an hour.

As the shuttle approached to pick us up, I noticed the old man sat in the front of the bus by himself, and this time, there wasn't anyone on the bus but my daughter and myself. I politely asked him where he was from, and he answered.

I said, "You are a preacher, aren't you?"

He looked at me with a puzzled look and said, "How did you guess?"

"God pointed you out to me. What brought you to Houston?"

He replied, "This is my last trip here. I came to get a final checkup. I am hoping I get a pass and will be told I am fine."

He seemed intelligent and shared a bit more. "I spoke at the First Baptist Church in Houston, Texas, a few weekends ago. There were thousands of people in attendance that Sunday."

How lucky am I?

I asked, "May I come and visit you later this evening and have you pray for me?"

"Yes, of course. You are welcome to come."

My mind began to think of how lucky I was to meet such a powerful preacher. I was more than lucky. I was blessed. God gave me another divine appointment. I waited until the evening and went to his condo in the motel. His beautiful wife answered the door. I told her I had an invitation to have her husband pray for me. She seemed a little reluctant to let me in, but Dr. Bailey Smith saw me. I am sure she was concerned he had already had a long day.

"Honey, this is Pam. I met her today on the van, and she wants us to pray for her."

It was an amazing visit with Dr. Smith. I know he told me several of his wonderful stories, as he was the pace setter for leading people to Christ. He told me his church had grown from 6,000 to 15,500 during his tenure. God openly blessed me with the opportunity He gave me to meet such a wonderful preacher man.

I look back on that night and know that while facing his own battles, he still had time for me. I felt chosen by God that he took the time to pray for me. I am not sure what the doctors told him on that visit to MD Anderson, but the Lord decided to call him home January 14, 2019, at the age of 79. I will always remember with fondness Dr. Smith and his very kind wife.

We left MD Anderson with no good news from the doctors, but I had been encouraged by those whom God sent to be with me during that time. Those people and their prayers have never been forgotten.

Chapter Eleven

As I faced this battle, God had brought to my mind some things He had asked of me when I was younger. It became clear as I pondered some of my memories and then lined them up with His Word and what He had told me.

When I was about 18 years old, I felt the Lord telling me to tell others about Him. I have always loved the church, and while I moved in and out occasionally with my closeness to God, I was sure of Him and He never moved from me. I wanted and needed to be obedient to His request, so I took a 5' x 7' sheet of plywood, wrote "Jesus Loves You" on it, and nailed it high up on a splintering telephone pole on a highly traveled highway.

I reflect now and think about what that meant. Jesus was nailed to a tree, held there with love, so we would know of His love for us. He was lifted high for all to see.

As thousands traveled by my homemade sign, some read it. Some were changed by it, and some didn't give it a second look. Maybe that is what we do to Jesus. We overlook and bypass Him at times. Sometimes we read His words or pray but quickly let the thought of Him vanish like a vapor, and sometimes—we are genuinely changed.

Then later in my life, while attending my home church, the Lord instructed me to rent a portable sign for the church and put announcements and Scriptures on it. I faithfully followed His instructions. Every Saturday night, I went to the church around dusk and would get my letters out and try to think of something that would bless people when they read the sign as they drove by.

I faithfully changed the sign every week, but there were times I didn't feel like doing it, or I couldn't think of what I needed to say on the sign. I never did tell anyone but the church secretary and one deacon that it was me doing it. I didn't want anyone at church to know what I was doing.

After one year, Saturday night rolled around, and so did my normal time to go to the church to change the sign. However, that night was different. It was bitter cold outside. I desperately wanted some help that night, so I ask my daughters if they would help me.

Their united reply was, "Momma, it's too cold. Just forget changing that sign tonight."

Well, I think they are right. I might get a cold from being out in the night air.

I walked into the kitchen, feeling released of my responsibility and not even thinking of God or the sign, and a voice said to me, "If you are faithful over a few things, I will make you ruler over many things."

Okay, God. I know that was You speaking to me, and I will go change the sign.

My girls thought I was crazy, and they still didn't want to help that night.

Before I left my house, I got out my letters for the sign and put some scripture together that I thought would bless someone the next morning. I definitely didn't want to be standing out in that cold air trying to think of what to post on the sign. When I finished, I went into the brisk night, got in my car, and headed to the church.

When I pulled up in the parking lot of the church, it was desolate. Normally, it was peaceful, and I actually enjoyed getting the sign ready. That night, at 9:30 p.m., it was late, dark, and bitter cold, and I was just getting started on the sign. I had to climb up on the sign, and by the way, it was not warmer up higher in the wind. I felt as if I would surely freeze to death! It always took me 30-40 minutes to climb up and place letters on both sides of the sign. Only God remembers what I put on the sign that night, but it was a night I will never forget.

Once again, though, I felt God wanted His name and Word both high and lifted up, just as He wanted when I nailed the sign to the pole on that highly busy highway years ago. God's will for me had not changed. I was to proclaim Him for others to see Him and believe in Him!

As I finished the sign in the miserable weather that night, I returned to the semi-warmth of my car. My hands felt as if they were blue from cold. I fumbled with the keys to get the car started, and as I did, I noticed something sitting on the curb beside my car that got my attention. It was a rather large bird, black and purple in color, with ice on its wings.

I have always loved birds, and I have fed them and watched them for years. They are beautiful to me, and I love the freedom they have when they fly. I love how God watches over each one of them.

Are not two sparrows sold for a farthing? And one of them shall not fall on the ground without your Father. But the very hairs of your head are all numbered. Fear ye not therefore, ye are of more value than many sparrows. – Matthew 10: 20-31

I rolled down my window, and the bird sat there looking up at me.

I spoke to the bird. "Little bird, are you sick? Why are you here all by yourself late at night?" As I spoke to the bird, it would turn its head to the left and to the right, as if it were trying to understand me. Then suddenly, it flew up in the air and left my sight.

When this happened, I heard God's voice audibly speak to me. He said, "I know what you do for me. You have faithfully changed the sign for a year without many people knowing, but I know what you do for me." I heard His voice clearly, as if He were sitting next to me in the car. I began to cry, and my car had the appearance of a cloud inside. It was the Holy Spirit.

I pulled out on the empty highway, crying and praising God all the way home. When I entered my home, Julie was awake. Julie asked me, "Mother, what is wrong with you?"

I said, "Oh, this bird..." Then I told her the story. My kids still remember the story to this day and kind of laugh because they think their mom is crazy. However, they also know that I know God!

To be honest, I had never heard of God audibly speaking to anyone. God knew that, so the next morning, as I sat on the back row in church, my pastor told a story.

"When I was a young boy, I was playing in the back-yard of our farm home. I was standing on a rock when God audibly spoke to me and told me I would be a preacher in the End Times." He said it scared him to death, and he ran into the house and nervously asked his mom, 'What is the End Times?' We had never gone to church when I was that young, so it was scary for me."

She replied, "Son, where did you hear that?"

He said, "I never told Mom that God had spoken to me aloud."

My pastor was involved in ministry for 60 years before he passed away. I knew when he spoke that morning what I heard was real. It was God who spoke to me that cold night, and the pastor confirmed it. I have no idea if I will ever hear God's voice audibly again, but I will never forget the night I heard God audibly speak to me.

Throughout my lifetime, God had asked me to make signs that lifted Him up. Therefore, when I was diagnosed with cancer, I prayed and talked directly to God and asked Him what could be done. He replied with an answer that remains sure and true. No doubt exists in my mind.

He said, "You can feel sorry for yourself or get people to pray, not a few but a multitude."

I wondered and asked God to explain. *Lord, it says in the Bible where two or more are gathered in thy name, there in the midst I will be. So why do I need a multitude?*

He replied, "People will pray for a while, and then they will get so busy with their lives that they will forget you, just like they forget me."

I pondered His reply to me, and it made sense. Even when others ask me to pray for them, I will pray and then I will forget because even I get busy with life.

God, I understand why I must get a multitude.

He said, "Keep yourself before people, and they will pray if you remind them."

After hearing God speak to me, the idea of the 3000 fliers was birthed. I told my daughter Shelly that I was going to make a flier and tell people my story—the story God gave me. I knew I was supposed to send it all over the United States. That may sound like a tall order, but He is a big God, and so we began.

We had pictures made and put a picture of me on the flier and a brief story about my diagnosis. At least, that is what we tried to do. Satan was tirelessly fighting Shelly each step of the way as she tried to get my picture and story to fit on the flier, but once again, God provided. Shelley's husband, Jacob, has always been skilled on the computer, and he was able to quickly and efficiently get the fliers completed and ready to mail. Getting the fliers out was exciting for me. It felt good to be obedient, and I immediately began to mail them to churches all over the United States.

Soon I began to hear from pastors, church members, and even church office support staff would call to tell me they were praying for me. I was overwhelmed at watching God's promise unfold. What a sight to see Him at work amid my darkest heartbreak and fear!

As powerful as those signs and fliers have been, God wasn't finished yet. I was traveling to Tahlequah, Oklahoma, when the Lord told me to get a billboard. He wanted me to use it to ask His people to pray for me. This was the third time He asked me to create a sign where He would be high and lifted up. Even though I would be asking others to pray for me, I remember what He said to me about getting a multitude to pray.

I knew I needed to be obedient, but I had one big problem. In my previous endeavors, I was able to make an affordable sign workable for what God had asked of me. This was different.

I knew I had to talk to God about my main issue. *Lord, those boards cost $500.00 a month. I surely can't afford to do that!*

He replied in a very simple but profound way. "Ask, and you shall receive."

I had used a billboard for my store for some time. The next day I called my rep, Jim D., who handled the account for my Amish store. I explained what was going on. "Jim, I can't afford a lot a month, and I can't sign a yearly contract. Do you think the company can help me with some kind of deal?"

He replied, "Let me see what I can do."

In two weeks, Jim came back with an answer for me. "We can give you three billboards to help your ministry without any cost except for the vinyl."

I was shocked. It was more than I even imagined, and I told him, "I can't believe it. The Lord has given me favor again."

I now have two billboards in Muskogee, Oklahoma, and one in Tahlequah, Oklahoma, with my picture on it, asking people to pray for a miracle for Pam Villines. The response has been overwhelming. In fact, two people in particular looked me up on the Internet to find out more about my story.

One was a man named Chris, an attorney from Dallas, Texas. He called me and said, "I saw your billboard. I looked you up and found your story. I want you to know I am praying for you!" He talked with me and encouraged me. About every two weeks he will call and tell me, "I'm praying for your healing miracle, Pam."

I told the billboard company, Headrick Outdoor Media in Laurel, Mississippi, that I will be a trend setter for them. "It won't be long, and many will put their prayer requests on billboards." I'm grateful for God and His Spirit who directs me.

The second person was a man who came into my store one day and asked for me by name. He said, "I saw your billboard, and I wanted to meet you." He brought me a handmade cross to wear. He said he had made it especially for me, and then he told me, "I'm praying for you every day."

Oh, the love I feel when God sends His people to me...

At the time of this writing, I am working on my next 2000 fliers to send out. This time they have a picture of me and my precious grandkids on the fliers. God has never told me to stop asking for prayer. I'm still trying to reach people, still believing, and still trusting in the miracle that so many are praying for me. I am still reminding the multitude that God is the Waymaker, even when it may appear there is no way. God's way is always enough. He alone is worthy of being high and lifted up, and I believe in miracles. I believe in Him.

I have been diligent to get the word out while trying to obey the Lord, just as I had been when He asked me to create the other signs. My heart's desire has been to reach people, as God had asked me to do. I have spoken in many churches, given out my cell number, and asked people to pray for me. Once someone has prayed for me, I asked them to text me afterward so I will know who has been praying for me and when they are praying. Each time I speak and share, a few sincere people from that church have texted me every day.

Chapter Twelve

I love going to church, and there was a specific Sunday that I was especially determined to be there. It seems like when I need church the most, Satan throws all he has at me to keep me away from church and God's people. On this particular Sunday, in February of 2019, it was no different. My road to church was paved with good intentions. I awoke early and was going to head into my Amish store to help cover for employees who had unexpectantly called in sick. I wanted to get to work, get my stuff finished, and then be in church service on time. I told my cook on the phone that I was going to church no matter what. I wasn't going to let anything stop me.

While trying to hurry and get to work, I felt God talking to me. The day felt unusual, and I didn't quite understand His closeness as I prepared to go to work.

Inside my car, I always listen to Old Dad Hagen preach, but today I turned him on my radio, and it wasn't long before I knew I needed to stop all my striving and rushing and simply pray.

I prayed for my children by name, and I asked God to put a hedge around their lives, to protect them, and I pleaded the Blood of Jesus over each one of them and my grandbabies, too. My family has always been important to me, and I knew that I must pray for them daily. As I prayed, I began to pray for my friends who texted me every day and told me they were praying for me. I prayed for those I could think of that needed the Lord's touch that day. I felt God in such a close way. I was close to Him, and He was close to me.

After I finished praying, I went to work at the store. I finished up all the necessary tasks, ready to leave for church when it was time. While I waited, a text came in from a girl who said she saw my face on a billboard. (I will explain later how that happened.) She wanted me to know God told her to pray for me and to keep praying. I looked her up on Facebook, and I was quite surprised. She seemed to be about twenty-four years old. I appreciated her message very much, but to be honest, I didn't get texts from people so young. I messaged back and told her I would be at my restaurant at noon.

She said, "I have never done anything like this, but God keeps bringing your name to me and telling me to pray for you."

Then I left and drove to Wagoner, Oklahoma, to Wagoner Assembly of God Church. As I drove, I pondered her remarks. I felt God holding on to me as if He was in the car with me. I walked into church, and they were singing praise and worship songs. I immediately fell into His presence. We worshiped for about thirty minutes.

I was sitting all alone, and there wasn't anyone close to me, but suddenly, I began to smell the most wonderful fragrance of sweet perfume. It reminded me of spring when all the flowers are in bloom, and you can smell the honeysuckle and other flowers in the air. The smell kept getting stronger and stronger. I looked around the sanctuary again to see if any woman was putting on perfume. Its scent was beautiful but overwhelming. There was no mistaking the sweet smell.

The smell triggered a memory of what my 80-year-old friend Dot told me about her healing. Dot had a brain tumor for months and was suffering from it. She prayed and prayed, and then one night she woke up and heard God say, "I am that I am." Then she smelled the sweetest and purest fragrance. It smelled like roses. She said she knew God healed her. *Can this be happening to me? Is the fragrance filling my pew actually God passing by and healing me?* Soon the pastor asked for those who needed something from God to come to the front of the church.

Many went forward and stood. I remained aware of Pastor Tim and his words, but I felt the Lord overwhelmingly prompting me to pray for the elderly woman standing next to me. I knew I had to pray for her, even though I desperately needed prayer. I placed my hand upon her and began praying for her aloud and asking the Lord to touch her and remove all fear from her. I prayed for ten minutes or so until she began to weep. She began to hold me, and I can honestly say, I never needed a hug more than I did that morning. It was like the Lord wrapping His arms around me. She felt the same way, and we held each other for the entire time. She began to pray for me and cry for the Lord to heal me. It was the sweetest prayer and time with God that I had ever had.

As the service progressed toward the ending, the pastor said, "I felt God in this place today. I smelled His fragrance just like He was walking the aisles in the church. When I had stage IV lung cancer, I went to Pensacola, Florida, to the Brownsville revival. When they gave the altar call, I went forth and God healed me of cancer right then and there. I smelled the same sweet smell here today that I smelled at that revival."

I knew then the strong fragrance I had smelled was the Lord passing by me where I was sitting. I am glad I went to church. I have pondered what happened and thought how blessed I was to be so close to God that morning. I believe He did a great miracle in me.

Never underestimate the Lord. I have gone to church all my life and never experienced anything like this. If you are sick and lonely and need someone to love you and hold you, remember there is God. He is faithful.

~

At times, I have been blessed to speak in various churches. One of the churches I spoke in was the First Baptist church in Muskogee, Oklahoma. I knew the pastor, Johnny Derouen, as he was a customer and came into my Amish restaurant to eat on occasion. When I was diagnosed with stomach cancer, I ask him to pray for me.

He said, "Sure. Come Wednesday night, and the church will pray." I knew he was sincere, and I wouldn't have missed going to church that Wednesday night.

When I arrived, the pastor warmly greeted me and let me know there was going to be a deacon's meeting. He said, "My wife will show you the way to the meeting. I'm going to have the deacons pray for you."

I expected to see five or six deacons, but when I entered the room, quite to my surprise I might add, there appeared to be about 25 men. I was shocked at the attendance and a little taken aback. Next the pastor introduced me, and I asked the pastor if he minded me addressing the men before we all prayed. He caringly and graciously allowed me to go ahead and share with them.

I proceeded to tell them my story and how God had asked me to get people to pray, not just a few but a multitude. I explained how I had been giving out my cell number and asked those people who prayed to text me. When I finished, the pastor said, "I'm going to do something in this church I have never done before." Then he picked up the Bible and started to read James 5:14-16.

Is any sick among you? let him call for the elders of the church; and let them pray over him, anointing him with oil in the name of the Lord: And the prayer of faith shall save the sick, and the Lord shall raise him up; and if he have committed sins, they shall be forgiven him. Confess your faults one to another, and pray one for another, that ye may be healed. The effectual fervent prayer of a righteous man availeth much.

After he finished reading, he took olive oil and placed some on his finger and touched my head. All the men gathered around me and began to pray. One man, a local physician, got on his hands and knees and prayed right in front of me. I felt God's presence as they prayed. *This pastor has basically laid down his life for me. He has never practiced this here before. What will his congregation think?* I will never forget that pastor who I felt willingly stepped over some unspoken, invisible line for me. The physician, whom I will call David, the one who got on his knees to pray, still texts me each day to tell me that he is praying for me. He has been praying for over a year a year and a half now, and he remains faithful to pray. When you get a diagnosis like mine, that simple but powerful text or call means the world.

God uses others to be an encouragement to me, and I am grateful. These men and that pastor stood in the gap for me. I will always remember and cherish that meaningful night.

~

I also had the opportunity to speak at Timothy Baptist Church in Muskogee, Oklahoma. The pastor, Kelly Payne, is another good friend of mine. When I texted him one evening, I asked him if I could give my testimony in his church at that night's service. He didn't hesitate and told me to come on over to the service.

I was scared because I spoke from my heart, no notes, nothing to prompt me. I shared my story, and I asked the congregation to pray for me. When I was through speaking, the pastor asked the church to come and pray for me. I must say that many came and laid hands on me for healing. I thought how awesome it was to have people who really cared for me. This blessing overwhelmed me and covered me.

I, again, gave out my cell number, and to this day, I have two faithful people who have never missed texting me to say, "I'm praying for you." There are several others who text me from time to time, but my friends and prayer warriors Richard Sam and Danita Jackson, who were at the service that night, never miss a day. What would have happened if they had chosen to skip church that night? I was glad God directed them to me, just as He had directed me to them. It was His divine plan for our paths to cross, even before the three of us knew it.

Since my journey of getting multitude to pray, I have been to Baptist, Pentecostal, non-denominational, and many different denominations of churches. I learned it is most difficult to get into a church to speak if the pastor doesn't know you. I understand and even appreciate how carefully a pastor must guard his pulpit. I also pray for the Lord to open doors for me to give God glory for His mighty work in my life. I must trust God, as He alone opens the doors, and I meet those He intends for me to meet on this path that He and I are walking together.

Chapter Thirteen

"James the Dreamer" is a pastor from Louisiana who sent me a message on Facebook. He said, "Pam, you do not know me, but I am a friend of yours on Facebook. You sent a letter to our church several months ago, and one of our members made copies and handed them out to church people to pray. We have been praying for you. That was several months ago, but last night I had a dream about you. I only know you by your picture on Facebook, but you came to me in a dream. You ask me to please pray for you, especially right now. I prayed with you, and then we prayed together. I have been a minister over 50 years, and I have never had God send me someone in a dream whom I have never met in person. All I know is your picture on Facebook."

I read every word the pastor texted me that morning, and I asked him to please call me. Later that evening, he did call me. When he heard my voice, which is very Southern, he said, "Your voice sounds exactly like the voice in my dream." In tears, he said, "I just can't believe God asked me to pray for you in a dream."

He told me that he has two sons in their twenties. They were in a serious car accident, and one of them died in the accident. The medical team on site revived him, but he suffered a traumatic brain injury, and he lives at home with them. The other son was traumatized and turned to drugs. It was so serious that he had to be placed in rehab for a period of time. With much hard work and God's grace, he appears to be doing better.

The pastor also said, "One day I got up to look out the window, and my son was hanging from a tree in the yard. I ran to help him and saved his life. I have had that reoccurring day of when I saved my son every night in my dreams until the night God brought your face to me to pray for you."

I was in tears as he told me the story. *God, you put me in this man's dreams to pray for me, but I believe I am to pray and be a friend to him, too.* God works in mysterious ways, including sending the pastor's fellow church member who called to say she prays for me every day!

The Spirit of the Lord is upon me, because
he hath anointed me to preach the gospel to

the poor; he hath sent me to heal the broken-
hearted, to preach deliverance to the captives,
and the recovering of sight to the blind, to set
at liberty them that are bruised, To preach the
acceptable year of the Lord.- Luke 4:18-19

~

I received a telephone call from a sister in Christ
named Lamesha Grimes, an evangelist from Colum-
bia, South Carolina. She left a detailed message on my
phone to tell me she practiced intercessory prayer at
her church with another woman in their congregation.
As Lamesha was going through the prayer requests, she
found my flier asking for prayer. She immediately felt
the Lord tell her to call me. She left me a voice message
that said she was calling to pray for me, and since she
didn't reach me, she would pray on the phone, and pray
she did!

When I listened to her message, I was overwhelmed
by her prayer-a prayer from this wonderful lady whom
I had never met. I had never heard anyone pray like she
did. She prayed for my healing, and she prayed for the
enemy to take his hands off me. She prayed for almost
fifteen minutes on the phone.

The next day I called her, and we spoke and laughed and talked about Jesus. One thing is for sure, Lamesha knows God!

As we talked that morning, she began to enter into prayer. When she finished praying, she began to sing in an African language and in Hebrew. She said the Holy spirit gave her the languages while in His presence. It was amazing.

Lamesha has been my encourager and stronghold. After we prayed, she offered to mail out 500 fliers for me, so I sent her the fliers. She has faithfully kept her promise to me to get people to pray for me. Even though I had only known her for a week when she stepped in to help me, I felt I had known her all my life.

Who delivered us from so great a death, and doth deliver; in whom we trust that he will yet deliver us:-2 Corinthians 1:10

Lamesha and I have become close friends now, sisters in Christ, and we talk weekly. She prays for me, and after she prays, she sings to God in the spirit. Some days when we talk on the phone, she can pray for hours.

One of the most enjoyable divine appointments has been a man named Charlie Soap. The first time I met Charlie, he had on a western hat with jeans. His hair was long and in braids down his back. He is a Cherokee and was married to the Chief of the Cherokees, Wilma Mankiller, who passed away.

Charlie has been a good friend to me and comes to see me at my Amish store. He is very spiritual, and we talk about God and the spirit man. He has asked many Native churches to pray for me. I have never met a man as full of God as Charlie.

He told me how he was going to build a fire for me and pray for me with eagle feathers. I believe Charlie Soap has a closeness to God that is very rare. He knows his culture well and serves people in need.

I am one of those he uplifts with prayer and confidence. I was raised among the Seminoles as a child, and I remember how they prayed and believed in God. The stomp dances they performed were most amazing. I often saw eagle feathers floating in the air, as the medicine man danced.

My granddaughter, who is six, met Charlie at the store one day. I said, "Lea, this is Charlie Soap. He is Native American." Then I took his ponytail and held it up for her to see. She was excited and ran to her father, telling him she had met a real Native American.

I felt Charlie was sent to me to pray for me. His culture and his spirit have a history full of God and helping others. I have always felt his sincerity, and I will always value my friendship with Charlie Soap.

> But they that wait upon the Lord shall renew their strength; they shall mount up with wings as eagles; they shall run, and not be weary; and they shall walk, and not faint.
> —Isaiah 40:31

I believe in divine appointments. I have sent out over 3,000 fliers to churches in the United States. I have met many friends who pray for me. I believe my whole life has been made up of divine appointments.

❧

So many people have become my spiritual advisors and prayer warriors, and my cousin Carolyn Nance has prayed many hundreds of prayers for me.

Another one of my divine appointments has been Ed Chaney, a Creek Indian who is a Baptist pastor and my very good friend. He is 82, and I have had many talks with him. I have always told him that he is in the box, never swaying to the right or left about his Baptist affiliation. He has dished it right back and given me a hard time about us Pentecostals who like to shout and speak in tongues. We have the utmost respect for each other, and maybe I have caused him to think a tiny bit out of his box because he asked me to buy him a bottle of anointing oil. I have laughed about that, and in my mind, I felt I have been making progress with Ed. I do not use the word friend lightly because a true friend is hard to find, and Ed is a true friend.

Carolyn, my sister in Christ, and her prayer warrior friends have been intercessory prayer warriors for many people throughout the years. When I first called her and told her of my diagnosis, she immediately began to pray, "God, incapsulate this cancer!"

She brought two young men with her to my store to pray with me. She said these two men ministered all over the world, proclaiming God to everyone. When they prayed, they ordered the cancer to be encapsulated, and I believe that is what the Lord did for a year. Carolyn has prayed many prayers for me, and I know she can reach God. Carolyn and her friend Linda recently visited me and prayed over me. Linda can sing in the Spirit, and she sang blessings over my life. These believers are the type of people to surround yourself with-people of faith!

Are you fighting a battle? Then find praying people who believe in God's miraculous healing and who will lay hands on you and pray for you.

...they shall lay hands on the sick, and they shall recover.—Mark 16:18

Chapter Fourteen

Recently, I woke up and it appeared I was feeling well, so I got ready for work. It was a typical day until I ate breakfast. Afterward, my stomach began to cramp, and I had to take a muscle relaxer to feel better.

The cramping can be partially controlled by the medicine, but the cramping is a battle cry, because when the cramping begins, the war rages. The enemy taunts me, reminding me that the doctors have told me that I am not well. He stands as my accuser, "Pam, you will never be well." Then the fear rises, trying to drown me.

How many of you can relate to fear? I can tell you—40 million of you. I pulled the statistics from the adaa. org website. I know JESUS said to fear not, not once, not twice, but 365 times! That is basically one "fear not" for each day of the year. Maybe that is another reason He wants us to rest in His Word daily?

> For I am sure that neither death nor life, nor angels nor rulers, nor things present nor things to come, nor powers, nor height nor depth, nor anything else in all creation, will be able to separate us from the love of God in Christ Jesus our Lord.—Romans 8:38-39

I know not to fear, but fear comes. When it does, these are the things I began to do: first, I plead the Blood of Jesus over my mind and body; second, in an audible voice, I say aloud that if I can hear my words, so can the devil. Then I tell Satan to flee, in the name of Jesus; third, I pray and remind myself that no weapon formed against me will prosper.

I'm fighting the enemy with God's Word, and by His authority, the enemy must flee from me. For surely, I will live and not die.

By His stripes, WE ARE HEALED! GOD is not a liar. His words are true, and He says we are healed, even if we have the tiniest mustard seed size of faith.

I know and understand there are thousands of people praying for me. Prayer changes things, and we know that because His Word says to pray, and I am living proof of those prayers. When it comes to faith, I have heard many people say, "I can believe for your healing, but I can't believe for mine!" It seems it is easier to believe and trust God on behalf of someone else. I'm believing and trusting God. He will not fail.

You may be starting to have doubt about your situation, or you may be in a complete free fall—an all-out panic attack. My solution when I find myself combating fear is to quote Scripture. Feed your mind truth. Get praise and worship music going. Find videos and shows and podcasts with your favorite pastor or evangelist. These are ways to beat the devil.

God did not put sickness in us; He didn't put it in me. I must not start blaming God. No good Father finds enjoyment in his child being sick. He wants us to be well and have blessings. God wants us to enjoy a happy eternity with Him, which is the ultimate joy He desires for us. He loves us and wants us to find our joy in Him, no matter what our circumstances may look or feel like. He is love.

It is important to remember that. You must know it deep in your soul, and you must hold on to that. Satan is no respecter of persons—child, adult, male, female, those in good health, or those who face a dark prognosis.

I have been serious about knowing God in a real way. In the middle of the night, while others sleep, Jesus—in His love—stays with me.

~

"Help us, Lord, to make it just one more day. When trials come, we feel so fragile, and we can't even think of making it one more day. You come and lift us up and carry us through the fire. You lift our burdens, and we fall to our face, not understanding you were with us all the time. You never left us to face heartaches and failures alone.

"You presented yourself when sickness came; You lifted us high above the dark valley. When we experienced grief and could not face the thought of losing someone close again, You comforted us.

"Lord, we questioned you when we experienced many failures. We could not understand how You would help us succeed. During those times when we felt anxiety and fear surrounding us, You made us strong instead of weak. As we confronted the situation, You helped us realize, we will not fail because of Your love and grace.

"We are amazed, Lord, how You have given us strength to overcome even the greatest giants in our lives. We never understood the total picture of what You have in store for us. We cannot understand why we must go through these difficult times. You remind us that You have never let us down, even in the most difficult situations. Lord, when we pray and it seems like nothing could happen, You surprise us and heal those whom we have prayed for.

"You have taught us to love others, and put them first, and by this, You heal our own broken spirits. You bless us with blessings of joy and happiness. We stand strong in Your mighty power as You deliver us from temptations of life. Lord, You give us hope, when it seems hopeless.

"You strengthen us when we are weak. When we fully understand that life is just a vapor passing so quickly, even the smallest things we do will be our rewards in heaven.

"You have made gates for us to travel. Even in our mother's womb, You made plans for us. You told us to love and be strong. When friends and family have left us all alone, You come to remind us to never give up!

"I have great and mighty plans for the future. When we fall flat on our face, You comfort us. When our tears come night after night and our best friend is far away, You reach down to help us and give us strength.

"Lord, I am amazed at how much You love us. No one understands how alone we have been-the emptiness we have tried so hard to hide, as we kept our secret tears inside. How can You love us like You do? We are amazed how much You care for us. We cannot understand, because we have let You down so many times. You took our sins away and made us whole and clean again.

"We are not afraid to face the problems of tomorrow. Although we struggle, we know You are with us. Your grace will be strong and not weak. In Jesus name."

Chapter Fifteen

This book is coming 17 months after I was diagnosed with a deadly stomach cancer. The doctors did not believe I would be here to write my story. Yet, here I am—book in hand—sharing what God has taught me on this precarious journey. Every medical person I have been in contact with looks at me with the same doubting look in their eyes. The looks are immediately followed up with an explanation that no one usually lives this long with my diagnosis. My prognosis seems somewhat unreal to me since I hadn't felt bad, and the cancer had been staying contained.

Three months ago, I went to the ER for what I thought was a basic kidney infection. The doctor insisted on a CT scan, which revealed I had diverticulitis. Whew! I was uncomfortable, but I was relieved to know what was going on. The doctor placed me on medication that I took faithfully for three weeks.

Unfortunately, nothing changed. My issues seemed to stay the same, and the cramping I felt did not stop. I found no relief.

My daughter Julie, the nurse, said, "Mom, you should be getting better." Fear knocked a little louder on the door, so I went back to the ER for more tests. This time the CT scan showed no sign of diverticulitis. However, the scan revealed the cancer had spread into my lower stomach.

As soon as possible, I went to my regular physician, Dr. Jay Geary. He carefully and methodically reviewed the information and recommended a surgeon whom he wanted me to see. He also mentioned that my appendix needed to be removed. *What in the world is going on?*

I have never felt more compassion from a physician than I have from Dr. Geary. He offered to pray with me, and I saw in his compassionate eyes that he cared for me as a person, not just a patient. His nurse Katie Bolen cried and prayed with me many times in the office. The Lord has always put His people in my pathway to encourage me.

Dr. Geary said, "Pam, you have done one thing, and you have put your faith in God and your trust in Him."

I replied and told him confidently that someday I will walk back into his office, and I will be healed. He told me that he will be waiting to see me.

Then Dr. Geary made me an urgent appointment with the surgeon. Julie and I got up the next day and went to his office. No doctor has better bedside manners than Dr. Geary.

The surgeon was the opposite. I didn't expect to hear what he said or how he said it. It was as if I had walked into the devil's playroom. This doctor was straight forward, and straight forward can be painful. "Pam, you don't have diverticulitis or anything wrong with your appendix. The cancer has begun to spread. There is nothing we can do for you, unless you want chemo."

I was sure that God didn't want me to take chemo. While I would never dream of offering advice to anyone else, I had heard from God on this matter. No matter how things looked to that surgeon, I chose God.

I politely thanked him, but I declined the treatment. He looked at me for a moment, and then he thanked me in return and left the room. That was that.

His words took my breath away. My heart wildly raced, and I felt engulfed in fear, as if I were smothering. I wanted to cry because I *truly believed* God had already healed me.

My heart was broken. My children's hearts were broken as well.

We all felt deflated, disappointed, sad, and let down.

The devil was not new at this game—the game of my life. He is an experienced accuser, always standing ready to pounce. He detected my fear, and he took my battle farther. Fear consumed me.

"Get behind me, Satan, you have no authority here! You will never win!" I began to send messages my close prayer warriors.

My friend Jim has prayed for me every day. Can you imagine praying for someone every single day? He is from Wagoner, Oklahoma, and we met at Wagoner First Assembly of God. We were both speaking at church that morning. He spoke first, sharing about his healings and the testimony of his seventy-seven years of life.

When I stood to speak, I noticed Jim filming me. I continued sharing my testimony, and after the service, he hugged me and told me he loved me. He has messaged me daily since we met. He encourages me by texting and seems so genuine when he tells me that God placed me in his life. From my side of looking at things, God placed him in my life. Every morning he has blessed me with a prayer and an upbeat message!

There have been times when I felt down. I have had times I felt all alone. When those moods have hit me, I have called my friends Mary and Richard, whom I have known for thirty years. They have been my unwavering prayer partners. We have attended church together for twenty-five years in Muskogee, Oklahoma.

I promised these two precious souls that I would be there for them in their later years. Richard celebrated his birthday of eighty years, and Mary is getting closer to that marker as well. These two people have been with me through some of my greatest and most tumultuous hurts. Now I'm in my sixties, and instead of me being there for them, they have continued to be here for me.

I told my sweet Mary I would always take care of her. Now I find myself in need of help, unable to help my friends as promised. They are steadfast and dedicated, and I know it to be true that when we walk through these dark times, we soon find out who our true friends are because of their actions.

God's people have mirrored His true love to me. The love and tenderness and care has blown my mind! My friend Bonnie from North Carolina, whom I met on the Assembly of God forum, has been a valuable intercessor for me. She has said, "Pamela, you are healed! God has this girl!" When I am battling in my mind, God sends people to call me and pray for me.

I have also met a new friend named Roberta Lock-hart who is eighty years young. She is a Southern sister in Christ, hailing from North Carolina. Wow! Wow! Wow! What a mighty prayer warrior! She is one of the strongest women I know. I wish I had an ounce of her faith. She told me God placed me on her heart, and she feels so close to me, that at times, she can feel my pain. No one has ever told me that. She takes God seriously, and she believes in Him for my miracle.

She has prayed, she has rebuked Satan, she has rebuked his attacks against me, and she has battled daily for me. She reminded me that we wrestle not against flesh and blood but principalities and powers. Stop and think about it. While anyone can see that I have a lethal battle raging in my flesh, God's Word says my battle is with principalities and powers, against the rulers of the darkness of this world, against spiritual wickedness in high places.

> For we wrestle not against flesh and blood, but against principalities, against powers, against the rulers of the darkness of this world, against spiritual wickedness in high places.
> Wherefore take unto you the whole armour of God, that ye may be able to withstand in the

evil day, and having done all, to stand.- Ephesians 6:12-13

Roberta called me as she often does, but she had a special message for me that day about a dream she had about me. She said it was rare for her to dream about anyone in particular. Then she asked me if I had heard of Katherine Kuhlman who was a female evangelist back in the day. In fact, I had heard of her. I read her books on healing and how God healed thousands of people through her.

In her dream, Roberta said she saw me standing in front of a pulpit, and people were being healed as they walked toward me for prayer. *That is my dream, that is what I ask Jesus for. I prayed to be healed and to be a walking testimony for Him. I want to see people get healed and delivered!* What a glorious testimony! I told Roberta how delighted I was that she had a dream involving me. I live for helping others know God, so her vision for me felt like God was reminding me that He still has plans for me!

Satan wants to tell people that they are too old or too sick or too "whatever" to be used by God. Don't buy into that nonsense. It is a lie from the pit of hell. Roberta spends much of her time driving sick people here and there. I'm sure God delights in watching her. She is a heroine to me, and I admire her. I hope I can become more like her, as she stays busy about Kingdom business.

There have been so many ... Debbie Bennett from Farmington, Missouri, has inspired me and challenged me to change my attitude. She has kept my thinking straight and on track. That has been significant as I have battled.

Bill Wilson is a good friend who has prayed with me, and he has stated firmly that I am going to be fine. He said the Holy Spirit told him so. He has been committed in lifting me up.

My friend Debbie Reece from Sweet Water, Tennessee, has been a lifesaver. She and her true-blue church ladies have prayed for me every week. Her prayers have lifted me up, carrying me through this hostile season. When I'm disconsolate, God brings her to my mind, and I call her.

All of us are in dogfights of some kind, and these are ways to fight the enemy:

1. Seek GOD and call on Him.
2. Call on those believers in Christ who you know will battle for you.

Another friend Beth is on a prayer team, and she is unending in her love of God. She is one of the sweetest sisters in Christ whom I have ever met. These last few weeks have been hard, and it is wonderful to hear from the Beth's of this world, especially my Beth.

~

Two months ago, I didn't believe I would be sick. The doctors told me I was, but it didn't seem true. Then I started having pain in my lower abdomen. For the last six weeks, I have been very ill—six weeks of the enemy tormenting me—six weeks of struggling to have faith—six weeks of the enemy fighting me in mind and body, every single day and every single long, quiet, scary night.

How do I handle it? I am a strong person. I must be for my children. If I get down, it is unnerving to everyone, and my children get down, too. I cannot let that happen.

When the battles have raged, I have prayed. When terror has closed in, the Holy Spirit has brought Scripture to calm my mind and heart. He has brought me truth. I have called the committed believers He provided as encouragers to lift me up—just as Aaron and Hur lifted the arms of Moses up when he became weary and started losing the battle.

But Moses' hands were heavy, and they took a stone, and put it under him, and he sat thereon; and Aaron and Hur stayed up his hands, the one on the one side, and the other on the other side; and his hands were steady until the going down of the sun.—Exodus 17:12

My flier made its way to Pastor Spencer from Little Rock, Arkansas. After he learned about me and what was going on, he sent me tapes of his preaching and singing, as well as singing by his talented wife. Pastor Spencer messages me every day. God's people hold my soul and heart up when they are heavy and want to collapse down.

~

Several months ago, I made my first Facebook video. I know that it takes millions of views to be considered viral, but I think 69,000 views within three months is still a multitude—God's multitude—God's praying people, praying for me.

God has orchestrated every person and every prayer that has been sent my way. He has not forgotten me. In sickness and in health, he has never left me or forsaken me. Believers have reminded me of His love with every prayer, call, and message.

Marty, a pastor, sent me this message after he received my flier, "Pam, just to let you know, our church is Atlanta, Georgia, is praying for you. I'm very much moved by your faith. I know God has raised you up for a national testimony of His power. You will stand before many and give God the glory. Because of your faithfulness, a national network will rise that will cause many to be converted and healed." May God bless Pastor Marty. I still believe his text.

The Lord knows this has been my dream. I have wanted and prayed for the Lord to use me in a way that brings Him glory. I have always wanted to tell people about God and His healing power.

Chapter Sixteen

Gloomy circumstances, a grave prognosis, fear raging and roaming all around? Stand your ground. Praise the Lord!

Because of my family history with cancer, I faced what I believed to be the toughest battle of my life the day my phone rang, and I received a cancer diagnosis. Little did I know the real battle would come when I started hurting and the pain would not stop. Pain is constant, taunting me.

Jesus prayed His cup would pass from Him. I have prayed this cup will pass from me. I need to be here for my children and grandkids. I do not want to miss a moment with them. I want to be at birthday parties. I want to see my grandchildren get married. I want to have tea parties with them and dance and talk to them about God. I will be a living testimony for Him. *Please,*

God, don't let me die. You see, it is important I stay here to pray for my children. If I should die, there will be no one to pray for them.

There is a delightful lady from Sweet Water, Tennessee, named Cindy, who has a lovely and compassionate spirit. She said, "Honey, I will pray for your kids every day if something should happen to you." What a phenomenal thing to do for me! Someone I have never met was sent by God to relieve my fears, to lift my weary arms.

It always seems when I have had rough days that God has sent reinforcements. In fact, God sent Leona and Judy from Fort Smith Assembly of God Church to lift me up. What would I have done and how would I have made it without the support of the multitude?

...so wilt thou recover me, and make me live.—Isaiah 38:16b

The LORD was ready to save me:-Isaiah 38:20a

Confess your faults one to another, and pray one for another, that ye may be healed. The effectual fervent prayer of a righteous man availeth much.—James 5:16

⁓

The foreboding battles have kept rolling in like storm clouds that are ready to burst. The enemy has been attacking me physically and mentally and emotionally. I have been doubled over in pain, often having to stay in bed because sitting has been too painful. My stomach is now distended and swollen, and now it is necessary to have my stomach drained.

One particularly bad episode found me buckled in pain. At just that moment, out of the blue, Ruth Wood from a small church in Okay, Oklahoma, whom I hadn't heard from in a while, sent me a text that said, "Pam, I know how nerve-racking fearing the unknown can be. It can cause us to live on pins and needles as we spend precious energy anticipating the worse case scenario. Continue your trust in our Lord for He is your strength. Please know I continue to pray and keep you in my thoughts daily."

Within one minute, I cried out to God, "Lord, look what You are doing, sending reinforcements in to help me!"

The next minute my phone rang, and it was Chris, an attorney from Texas who had learned about my illness and my need for prayer. His text said, "We love you, sister. Be strong in the Lord. Joy comes in the morning."

God, there are times I don't understand this journey—all the whys. Why do I have this disease? Why am I walking through this deep and treacherous valley? Why can't I come out of the valley, God? How long is all of this going to last?

> The LORD shall fight for you, and ye shall hold your peace.—Exodus 14:14

I have to believe this.

~

Luke Garrett is a man from Decatur, Arkansas, whom I met several months ago on Facebook. He called to pray for me. I looked up his profile. He had long hair, and I thought he resembled how I envision Jesus. He was a powerhouse when he prayed. I asked if I could come and speak at his church, so he arranged everything. I really wanted to go and share with his church family. However, I had felt worse each day. I wasn't sure I could drive that far, as it was quite a distance.

I asked God to help me. I know nothing is impossible with God. If He wanted me to go, He would make a way. He could give me the strength that I would need.

I wasn't sure what would happen as the time grew closer. The night before, I prayed earnestly. I awoke early the next morning and prayed again, "God, give me strength if You want me to go."

God not only provided my strength, he provided my friend and travel companion Roger. Roger is not a morning person, and really, unless he goes with me, he isn't too much of a church goer. He has always been a friend, and he put my needs above his own. I put on my red lipstick, we got in the car, and made the long drive.

Believe it or not, I had no idea what type of church we were going to, but I had been anticipating a miracle that day. God made a way, and I trusted Him. His ways are higher than mine, and I knew He had a reason and a plan.

It was sunny when we arrived in Decater, Arkansas. The air was crisp and clear early that morning. We found the church, and as we were going in, we were greeted warmly by a friendly and nice man. I asked about Luke, explaining that we were supposed to meet him. He said that Luke was inside the church teaching.

We quietly slipped into the back of Luke's class. Luke was on fire for the Lord! *He needs to be a preacher!*

Soon a young man tapped me on the shoulder, leaning in to ask me, "Do you know what the agenda is for today?"

"No. I am not sure if I am speaking or if I am going to be prayed for today."

He said, "Well, our pastor is in the emergency room with back pain so after this song, you have the pulpit."

Lord, you orchestrated this. I was supposed to speak. If the pastor had been there, my testimony time might have been shortened.

I spoke from the heart, sharing what I believe God wanted me to say. I have never used notes because I wanted the Lord to guide me.

The people listened as I told them of God's divine appointments. My divine appointment had happened that very day. I was to be prayed for, and I wanted to let God be God.

I loved those people. They poured out their hearts as they prayed for me. I felt such a love from them. More than one person told me they believed I was healed already.

After church, the enemy made my stomach hurt again. Satan could not stand the fact that I made it there. I hadn't quit. God was there, and people were blessed. The enemy hated that God was the most high and powerful!

God, please help me, Lord! You know my every thought Lord; you know all my needs. Lord, if I have done anything wrong in my heart that I have not ask forgiveness for, please forgive me. God, I'm still believing, and I want everyone to see that You, God, are still a miracle worker.

My path has been paved with the prayers of God's people, people like Dexter and Carol Payne—treasured friends who have prayed without ceasing for my healing.

Sheridan Gilbert has probably mailed me twenty cards. Each and every card has meant so much to me. I have always known she has been here for me.

People like Pastor Luke Yohannan and his wife from New Life Pentecostal Assembly in Oklahoma City, Oklahoma have prayed for me. He is from India, and at the time of this writing, his church has been fasting and praying for me. I was moved as the pastor wept and prayed over my life. He knows God, and he is a righteous man.

Connie Pippen from Bossier City, Louisiana, will soon be driving to Muskogee, Oklahoma, to pray for me. I am not sure if she has understood what an encouragement that has been to me. I have cherished knowing that we will meet in person soon. Even during this pain, God has sent hope and friendship. Looking forward to meeting Connie is a gift in itself.

Stephanie Pappas Stetson from Texas is a friend who messaged me about four months ago. "Pam, I coming to pray for you." That seemed unbelievable. It was a five-hour drive. She reflected love and compassion and has ministered to me greatly. In fact, she has now come three times. This is above and beyond what anyone could ask of another person.

I can only imagine what a crown she will receive from God for her obedience. I cried as I sat there thinking of her and her ministry.

She never asked for a dime, and she paid for her motel room. I bought her dinner, and we went back to the room and listened to praise and worship music before she began to read Scriptures to me about healing. Then she laid her hands upon my stomach and spoke over me. Her hand was hot at times. I believed God was healing me, but the next day, I was still struggling.

Lord, your will be done.

There are so many people I know and love—so many whom God has sent—that my concern has been leaving people out of this book who have been very near and dear to my heart—people such as all the friends from my hometown. Please know that all the messages and texts and prayers have meant everything. As I have fought this battle, I may not have every name in place, and please forgive any errors, but be assured, you are etched forever in my heart, and God remembers and knows every single prayer prayed.

As much as I have wished God would light my entire path now, He lights just enough path for me to take the next step, so I have walked by faith.

I don't know how long I can maintain my present condition. I don't know how long my Jesus will position me on this earth, but I do know that God has all control. I know He loves me and you. I know God was not caught off guard. I know He knows my situation, and I know I believe in Him for my miracle.

The greatest walk is in the healing hands of Jesus. I pray He will heal my body, and I will tell the world about His mighty miracle.

God, You are not a respecter of persons. You said by Your stripes we are healed. I stand and I believe. I don't care what the doctors tell me, but Jesus, please help me keep my faith. I struggle so from day to day. I will fight the enemy. I WILL TELL HIM TO LEAVE! He does not belong here. I plead the blood of Jesus over my life. Satan has no authority in my home or my children's lives, and he has to go! In Jesus' name.

∽

I stay at home now, always in pain. I have prayed for what feels like my entire life for God to give me a ministry, but I never thought this would ever happen to me or this would be my ministry. I know when He heals me, there will be many gathered to hear my testimony. I will honor God with all my heart and all my mind and all my strength.

The pain has felt unbearable at times. My stomach has remained swollen. The misery has never ceased. I haven't been able to eat or drink, although I have tried to force myself.

One night, at about 3:00 a.m., I woke up, still in severe pain. I got up and took a morphine pill, hoping to sleep. By 5:30 a.m., I felt like I was out of my head. I was sobbing and could not stop. I saw a vision of something that I felt might have been the Lord. I spoke three times to the Lord and told Him that I wasn't ready to go.

Then Satan came to me, hatefully accusing me of past wrongs, throwing my sin in my face. He told me that I was not going to heaven. He was more evil and wicked and mean than I had ever thought about him being. I discovered what kind of wicked enemy he is—truly the accuser of the brethren.

I told him no! God will forgive us of any sin when Jesus is our Lord.

God came again, and He told me that all will die unless they go in the Rapture. When death comes for us, no one will have time to confess. The Lord told me that we must be ready to stand before Him at all times.

This vision unnerved me. My heart broke as Satan reminded me of my sin. I cried when I relived my sin, but I am firmly planted in knowing I am forgiven. That is truth.

Chapter Seventeen

I have gone through so much. There have been many highs and many lows. Over the last few weeks, right before this book will go to print, things have changed again.

I told my daughter that I needed to use the restroom, but I kept having difficulty. My daughter, the nurse, felt I might have a bowel blockage. Therefore, she thought we should go directly to the emergency room. I agreed and we went straight to the hospital. I was nervous and apprehensive about the trip.

After I was examined, the doctor came out and told us that I did, indeed, have a partial blockage. He sent us to St. John's Hospital in downtown Tulsa, Oklahoma. I hate hospitals, and this was worse because I didn't know what to expect. I put my need for prayer on Facebook, having explained my circumstances and asked people to pray for me, while we waited on a doctor to come in for a visit. Later that evening, a nurse practitioner came by and shared her fear that the cancer had started blocking my bowels. She gave me a very bleak and grim outlook. She said, "You won't be able to have more than one surgery to fix your bowel, should it become completely blocked. If it blocks a second time, there is nothing we can do to help you." This young woman in her thirties wept profusely as she told me that I could die. She cried for thirty minutes, standing there in my room.

I stood up and hugged her as I said, "Honey, don't ever be ashamed to cry tears for someone like me. Your compassion shows, and I appreciate your concern." Then I told her how God told me to get others to pray—not a few but a multitude. I shared with her that I probably have over 100,000 brothers and sisters in Christ praying for me because God had so faithfully put me in the hearts of His people.

She said, "I will never forget your story, and I will pray for you." As she left, I was amazed that God sent such a caring woman to talk with me.

The nurse who was assigned to me was named David, and we immediately bonded. We laughed and I shared my story with him, and he loved me. When I was discharged, he said he would come and see me at my restaurant in a couple of weeks. He hugged me and prayed for me.

Everywhere I have gone, God has placed people in my life to encourage me. When I was released, I came home and felt better until I drank Ensure, which made me ill. I threw up and was sick most of the night. My daughter Shelly and son Mike stayed by my side. The next morning, people began calling me at 7:00 a.m. to pray for me. How they knew I was in distress, only God knows. I had ten intercessory prayer partners who called and prayed for me early that morning after being so sick. Some were people whom I had never spoken with before. I called three people in whom I have great confidence, and God began to speak and minister to me.

I know that my situation looks bleak. I have been told that if my bowel blocks fully, I most likely will die. My daughter Julie was worried when she came to see about me.

"Mama, if you start throwing up, we will have to go to the hospital, and they will admit you as an emergency patient. You will have to have your colon redone and possibly a colostomy."

I said, "Devil, I'm done. You will not put this on me. I rebuke you in the name of Jesus. You have to flee. God, I can't do this." I stopped throwing up and drank my water without any problems after I got a call from my friend Debbie Reese, the one from Sweetwater, Tennessee.

"Pamela, it is Satan. Rebuke him. Don't you give in. You have come too far to allow him to win. Get your faith together." I call Debbie my fighter because she pushes me to be motivated and not give up. I got my thoughts together and began to go one more round to fight and win this battle.

Then my phone rang, and it was Debbie Stephens, a woman from Goldonna, Louisiana. I had never spoken with her previously. She said, "Pamela, you don't know me, but I got your story off Facebook. I have been crying for days. My heart has been broken for you. I have prayed and prayed for your healing. I feel everything you are going through. You see, I was sick for one year with a stomach disorder. I was dying and no one knew what was wrong with me. I could not eat. My stomach would not digest. Finally, on my deathbed, I told God I was done. I could not do it anymore. The next day, the doctor came in and said they were going to try one last test on me. At the last minute, when my life was almost gone, the doctors found a solution to fix my stomach." She witnessed to me. She told me she loved me, and I believed her because my pain was her pain. I am ever so grateful that God placed her in my life. She will come and see me very soon.

I am still saying, "God, thank you for my miracle. I will live and not die, but God I need you and the miracle to manifest. I am almost to the point I can't make it, but I am believing for this miracle. God, it's in Your hands and Your control, but Lord, it isn't about me. It is about the multitude of people who have prayed and believed that I will have my miracle." This will increase the people's faith that God still does miracles.

God always makes a way, and this book has been something I knew He wanted me to share with others. I live a life full of passion for the Lord, a life revolving around my precious children and grandchildren, and a life that will never end because God chose me, and Jesus is my Savior. I am truly the child of the King.

As I look back at all of those who have prayed, I must share more about my Amish friends. Imagine my surprise when fourteen Amish people showed up at my door to tell me they loved and to pray for me, even their 90-year-old grandmother. We laughed about all the years we have worked together and how far we had come. I was grateful they showed me love and respect. We are family.

Because of my God-given ideas, all the multitude is my family. God placed them in my heart. "God, give us our miracle and show the world that You still do miracles."

I have made new spiritual families and found new love from people I would have never met in other circumstances. These have been people who have changed my life forever. I have seen God's hand at work. I have appreciated those 70,000 views on my Facebook video who have represented real people and prayers.

> "God, the ending is Yours, Lord. What will be is up to You. I hope, Lord, that I never disappointed You. I am not claiming perfection for myself, Lord, but I have tried to live a good Christian life, but You know how many times I fell on my face. Those times, Lord, I ask You to forgive me, remembering when we fall short, You will always forgive us."

For verily I say unto you, That whosoever shall say unto this mountain, Be thou removed, and be thou cast into the sea; and shall not doubt in his heart, but shall believe that those things which he saith shall come to pass; he shall have whatsoever he saith.—Mark 11: 23

I will continue to choose to speak to the mountain. I pray that you, as part of the multitude, will continue to

pray. I love each one of you, and I still wear red lipstick
every day.

From Start to Finish

I am not one to believe in coincidence. God has His mighty hand upon us, and He has a plan for us. Many times, God has brought someone through the door of my Amish store with His plan in mind. Some come through for a good meal. Some are curious. Some come through and want to pray for me. Some come through, and I am able to offer prayer. The store has a ministry within the walls that only God could orchestrate.

In 2015, a husband and wife came into my store for breakfast. They were an older couple, very friendly. As our conversation progressed, I mentioned I wanted to write a book titled *The Red Lipstick Diaries*, based upon some past hurts I suffered in church and my signature red lipstick I have always worn. Imagine my surprise when the gentleman handed me a business card that said he was the founder of a publishing company.

He asked me to call his office the following week to discuss my book idea. I knew I would need help writing the book. I am a wonderful communicator, but writing is something I struggle with, partly due to my busy schedule. It takes time to write and rewrite, and I had a lot on my plate already.

My mind turned all of this over throughout the weekend, and the following week, I called and left a message. After multiple conversations, spreading out over several months, I made a decision to wait. God had not given me His approval to start, as much as I wanted to have the book written and in production.

Although I never published through his company, that connection led me to another writer, and God allowed me to have my book written.

In His wisdom, He delayed my book because my book had changed. If I had written my story three or four years earlier, it would have been more a tale of hurt, but now my book is a tale of victory. The church is the Bride of Christ, and His bride has lifted me up many times over this last year and half.

That publisher was not the publisher for me, but that man was part of God's plan. God knew who and what I would need, and the groundwork was laid years ago for the book you are now holding in your hands.

~

Recently, I needed fluids. That meant a trip to the emergency room. While I was there, the doctor reluctantly did another scan on me. He was very skeptical about my blockage being gone. In fact, he was sure it would be worse. However, my son-in-law was with me, and he asked the doctor to proceed with another scan, even though it seemed pointless to the doctor.

We all know God doesn't work according to our human opinions—not even doctors' opinions. God works according to His plan. Imagine that doctor's surprise when he saw that my blockage was gone! Praise Jesus, for He is worthy of all praise!

While still at the emergency room, I received a call. A woman named Carla was on the phone, and she said she was calling me as promised. I have been taking medication, and to be honest, I simply couldn't recall her.

She asked what I was doing, so I explained that I was in the emergency room. She replied, "I am sorry to hear that. You and I are very similar. We have both gone to church all our lives. We raised our children and worked in church. We sacrificed to help others. We are good people."

I pondered what she said. I have not been able to help but wonder why I am going through this. What have I done or not done to deserve this pain I have been in?

I then asked her what has been wrong with her health. She began to tell me she had surgery on her brain, and she could only sit up in bed. Her life was drastically changed from being able to work to only being in bed. She shared with me that the doctors needed to perform more testing, but she has been afraid of the testing because it will be so close to her brain.

God, where are you?

Everything she had been saying, I had been thinking about myself. My heart poured out to her. Sometimes, when we are in a trial, we can only see what we are going through. It is natural and easy to become focused on our own problems and issues. We may forget that others are going through life experiences that are just as bad as ours—some even being worse! I cried for this woman. I felt her compassion for me, and I had compassion for her.

Let us lift others up! *God, if you give me my miracle, then I can go to her and tell her, 'Look! Jesus healed me!' God is no respecter of persons. He can heal you, too!*

My hope is to encourage others. I want to give them hope and life in the Word of Jesus! No matter what happens, I am healed in the name of Jesus!

Pastor Roy Smart called me this very morning just as I have been closing out writing my book. He has been a minister his entire career. He told me his church was having a prayer meeting for me today through Facetime. Several ladies prayed for me and the pastor. Then he said, "I don't know you, but God has put you in my heart to pray for you every morning when I wake and at night. I can't get you out of my heart! That is no accident. God is going to heal you and use you. When God places someone in someone's heart, He has a reason and plan. I believe you are going to be healed!"

I said, "We all have divine appointments with God!"

I pray you enjoyed my book. Know it has been from my heart and from my life. You have been divinely placed to connect with me. God has given us this divine appointment to meet here within these pages.

May God bless you and richly bless your life.

Love,

Pam

CPSIA information can be obtained
at www.ICGtesting.com
Printed in the USA
LVHW080152010719
622824LV00003B/5/P